Getting Numbers You Can Trust

GETTING NUMBERS YOU CAN TRUST
The New Accounting

A Harvard Business Review Paperback

ISBN 0-87584-290-9

The *Harvard Business Review* articles in this collection are
available as individual reprints. Discounts apply to quantity
purchases. For information and ordering contact Operations
Department, Harvard Business School Publishing Division,
Boston, MA 02163. Telephone: (617) 495-6192, 9 a.m. to 5
p.m. Eastern Time, Monday through Friday. Fax: (617)
495-6985, 24 hours a day.

Contents

We don't have the accounting concepts we need

Robert N. Anthony

Accounting doesn't really have a satisfactory conceptual framework – a broad outline of what financial accounting practices should be. And none of the groups that have taken on responsibility for articulating the framework has been able to do so. First the Committee on Accounting Research and then the Accounting Principles Board tried and failed. The latest attempt was made by the Financial Accounting Standards Board, a private-sector body with seven full-time members, charged since 1973 with developing the individual standards that govern financial statements.

The FASB spent 12 years and several million dollars trying to construct a general theory of accounting. But it has also failed. Published in six statements from 1979 to 1985, the latest conceptual framework only perpetuates – and at times even regresses from – current practice. (See the insert for an outline of the FASB concepts statements.)

Given the record of its predecessor organizations, I congratulate the FASB for actually producing something. The process is painful, so painful that many accounting and business professionals think we should put aside the issue of a framework and focus on solving particular problems to get a more immediate payoff.

One reason that practical people – whether they're accountants, financial analysts, or business executives – feel this way is that they are uneasy about the development of concepts. They understand how a particular accounting standard will affect their work; a standard helps solve specific business problems in a very direct way. These people have difficulty, however, understanding how a concept can affect them or their businesses. So they argue either that we don't need to worry about a statement of concepts or

Robert Anthony is the Ross Graham Walker Professor of Management Control Emeritus at the Harvard Business School. A member of the Financial Accounting Standards Board concepts task force since its organization in 1974, he has written widely on the subject of accounting, including six articles for HBR. His most recent book (with Charles A. Anderson) is The New Corporate Directors *(Wiley, 1986).*

that we can go slower in the process of conceptual development. Although they generally won't oppose the discussions, neither do they support them enthusiastically. Moreover, practical people tend to be bored by what they consider to be an academic discussion of ideas.

> *"There are only a few fundamental issues in financial accounting. The FASB ducked them all."*

The discussion is not academic. Standards are developed within the framework provided by concepts. Unsatisfactory concepts lead to unsatisfactory standards. In its recent exposure draft, "Accounting for Income Taxes," for example, the FASB specifically ducks the question of whether the amount of deferred tax liability should be discounted. It does so because its concept relating to the measurement of liabilities is silent on this topic. The question must be addressed sometime down the road; it is quite possible that when it is resolved, difficult and incomprehensible adjustments will have to be made to financial statements. How much better it would be if there already were a concepts statement that showed a way of resolving the issue.

Financial accounting reports are governed by generally accepted principles, or standards, which are derived from a conceptual framework. Accounting needs this framework for the same reason a country or state needs a constitution to guide the development of its laws (although the accounting framework does not have the legal force of a constitution). Without it, debate over the issues bogs down because arguments are based on individual frames of reference that are rarely made explicit, with no common basis for analysis. If some geologists accept the concept of

GOLDEN PARACHUTE APTS.

D.Fradon

evolution and others do not, arguments about the significance of a certain fossil formation are likely to get nowhere.

In this article, I will look more closely at why the board's statements fail to do the job, why a better way is needed, and what an effective set of guidelines might look like. Rather than analyze each statement separately, I will frame my discussion around the broad issues that underlie the construction of a framework: the central focus of accounting, the definition of key terms, the concepts of measurement and recognition, and the criteria for applying the concepts to standard and individual transactions. These correspond closely, though not exactly, to the topics established at the inception of the FASB's project. Examining them will help explain why the FASB has, however unintentionally, created confusion instead of clarity, controversy instead of cohesion.

Primary focus

Accounting must have a central focus. Since the debit-credit mechanism on which it is built necessarily makes accounting an articulated system, the parts of the systemic whole must be internally consistent. Until about 1930, the focus was on "stewardship." Accounting's principal purpose was to report how well a company's management had discharged its responsibility for safeguarding the company's assets. This naturally led to an emphasis on the balance sheet. Then the focus shifted toward the notion of "decision usefulness," with an emphasis on the income state-

ment. The popular use of "bottom line" to mean the net result of almost any activity testifies to the impact of this shift.

The FASB's Statement No. 1 codifies this change: "Financial reporting should provide information that is useful to present and potential investors and creditors and other users in making rational investment, credit and similar decisions....The primary focus in financial reporting is information about an enterprise's performance provided by measures of earnings and its components." In other words, measuring earnings, or net income, on the income statement should take precedence over measuring assets and liabilities on the balance sheet.

This is an excellent beginning, but it is only a beginning. Because most accounting controversies center on how to measure events that should be included in a period's net income, concepts on these matters are necessary. Statement No. 3 purports to define the "elements" of financial statements, but net income is not included.

Instead, the board introduces the concept of "comprehensive income," which is simply the change in equity from nonowner sources during an accounting period. Comprehensive income is a meaningless term. I have not seen it before and I doubt that I will see it again. Statement No. 3 ducks the debate on net income, saying that earnings are part of comprehensive income but *which* part is "as yet undetermined." Without determining which part, the FASB's definition will not calm any controversy.

Liabilities and equity. Statement No. 3 defines equity as the difference between assets and liabilities and comprehensive income as the change in equity from nonowner sources during an accounting period. This treatment makes equity a residual and requires that a sharp line be drawn between liabilities and equity. The FASB statement, however, does not draw this sharp line. It says only that equity refers to owner interests while liabilities refer to nonowner interests.

The FASB's distinction between the two terms is based on what is known as the proprietary theory of accounting, which practitioners have largely discarded in favor of the entity theory. The proprietary approach creates problems in the treatment of convertible debt, redeemable preferred stock, compensation in the form of stock options, deferred income taxes, noncash dividends, and donated property. The entity theory does not need to draw a sharp line between equity and liability to measure income. It treats funds provided by owners, or equity investors, as only one source of the entity's capital.

By far the most important conceptual issue in accounting relates to interest on equity capital. Under the proprietary theory, equity interest is not an expense. The entity theory, on the other hand, recognizes that capital always has a cost, even when it's from equity investors. Statement No. 3 mentions this topic in a footnote but does not address it, and the board never brings it up again.

The board clarifies the concept of net income somewhat in Statement No. 5 by stating that net income should be based on the idea of financial capital maintenance; that is, net income measures the excess of revenues of the period over the relevant expenses, and an entity has not maintained its financial capital unless this amount exceeds zero. The concept of financial capital maintenance is sound. The FASB, however, says that this idea underlies current practice, which is not the case. In current practice, equity interest is not recorded as an expense. Clearly, an entity has not maintained its capital unless its revenues are sufficient to cover this expense. Economists recognize this fact and regard the omission of equity interest from the accounts as one of the basic defects of current accounting practice.

Nonbusiness entities. With Statement No. 4, issued in December 1980, the FASB accepted jurisdiction for developing standards for nonbusiness entities. The statement asserts that accounting's principal focus for business enterprises differs from the focus for nonbusiness organizations. In making this distinction, the statement identifies three distinguishing characteristics of nonbusiness organizations: they do not have transferable ownership interests, their purpose is something other than making a profit, and they receive contributions (which the board thinks are different from revenues arising from the sale of goods and services). The remaining 50 paragraphs of the statement elaborate these characteristics and discuss their implications for financial reporting objectives.

It is difficult to find significant differences between business and nonbusiness organizations in these paragraphs—differences that affect the way they should account for their transactions. That nonbusiness organizations have no transferable ownership interests doesn't mean they need different accounting standards; it means only that they don't have to account for dividends and other transactions with equity investors.

In the same way, just because a nonbusiness organization doesn't have to make a profit doesn't mean it should not measure net income. A business entity measures its financial performance as the amount by which its net income exceeds zero. A nonbusiness entity measures its financial performance by the extent to which its net income is approximately zero. If it reports, on average, a large amount of net income, it has not used its resources for their intended purpose. If, on average, it operates at a deficit, it will eventually cease to exist—just like a business. My point is that the accounting concepts are the same.

The alleged difference relating to contributions has led to erroneous conclusions about this so-called element, which I shall discuss later. In my view, the FASB has overdrawn the differences between business and nonbusiness accounting and created unnecessary problems for itself and for the preparers and users of financial statements.

Defining elements

Statement No. 3 defines ten "elements" of financial statements for business enterprises. Two of these are investments by owners and distributions to owners; two others, assets and liabilities, are definitions. The remaining six are names given to relationships derived arithmetically from these two definitions. Statement No. 3 says that equity is the difference between assets and liabilities, comprehensive income is the change in equity from nonowner sources during an accounting period, revenues and gains are additions to comprehensive income, and expenses and losses are decreases in comprehensive income.

The only difference between revenues and gains is that revenues relate to major operations while gains relate to peripheral ones. The distinction between expenses and losses is just as superfluous—there is little justification for making it. Revenues and gains alike add to income, and expenses and losses alike reduce income. The only two definitions in this statement that matter are those for assets and liabilities. The others follow as a matter of elementary-school arithmetic.

Assets and liabilities. Statement No. 3 defines assets as "probable future economic benefits" and liabilities as "probable future sacrifices of economic benefits." It then waffles by saying that these conditions are necessary *but not sufficient* to classify an item. In other words, no item can be an asset unless it has probable future economic benefits, but not all such items are assets. The statement terms this difficulty in classifying assets "the problem of recognition" and leaves it at that. The board addresses the matter again in Statement No. 5, but it never resolves the problem.

This is a cop-out. It is no more helpful than defining voters as adult human beings. All voters are adult human beings, but aliens, felons, and certain other adults are not voters. Unless an accounting definition indicates both the necessary *and* the sufficient conditions for classifying an item in the accounts, it is inadequate. This is a fundamental rule of taxonomy. Under the board's definition – and without further clarification – the value of an organization's reputation or even its trademarks could be assets. Few accountants would consider this a good idea.

> ## "The FASB's definitions don't jibe with balance sheet numbers."

Moreover, these definitions don't jibe with the numbers on a balance sheet. Although the amounts reported for cash, receivables, and other monetary assets are indeed the estimated amount of their "future economic benefits," the amounts for nonmonetary assets have no necessary relation to benefits. The amounts for nonmonetary assets are essentially costs that are to be charged as expenses of future periods in order to achieve the central focus of accounting, the measurement of net income. Similarly, the amounts reported for certain liabilities, such as deferred income taxes, are not the amount of obligation.

Equity. Defining equity as the difference between assets and liabilities perpetuates an unrealistic concept that is prevalent in both textbooks and practice. The amounts reported as equity in a business entity are actually the amounts of capital obtained from two quite different sources: investments by equity investors and the entity's profit-making activities. In present practice, they roughly correspond to paid-in capital and retained earnings, respectively. None of the concepts statements makes this important distinction.

Nonprofit elements. When the Governmental Accounting Standards Board was established, the FASB's responsibility was limited to nongovernment entities. The FASB acknowledges this in Statement No. 6 by changing the term "nonbusiness" used in earlier statements to the narrower "nonprofit." (Actually, it uses the archaic "not-for-profit," which I will not perpetuate here.)

The FASB asserts that there are three distinguishing characteristics of nonprofit entities. Two, the absence of transactions with owners and the profit motive, do not require different elements. The third, contributions, does. In dealing with this and other matters, Statement No. 6 has become some 60 paragraphs longer than the earlier Statement No. 3, which

it replaces. Much of this growth is indefensible. The board has used the space simply to create new names for exactly the same definitions given in the earlier statement.

In developing a conceptual framework for accounting that applies to both types of organizations, there is an obvious advantage in drawing distinctions only between those features that truly make a difference. Users then don't have to learn two sets of accounting standards, and preparers don't have to decide whether an organization is or isn't a business enterprise.

Statement No. 3 recognized the elegance of such simplicity. In it, the FASB said it saw no reason to define assets and liabilities differently for business and nonbusiness organizations and that it expected that the definitions of equity, revenues, expenses, gains, and losses would fit both. It broadened the definition of revenues to include inflows from donor contributions. It even changed the term "owners' equity" used in a preliminary exposure draft to the broader "equity."

In a striking return to obfuscation, Statement No. 6 disregards the FASB's previous attempts to promote commonality. It uses "net assets" instead of "equity," and "changes in net assets" instead of "comprehensive income." Here the board is playing word games. The definitions of these new terms are identical to the old ones – the same arithmetic derivations from the definitions of assets and liabilities.

To make matters still more confusing, Statement No. 6 introduces the term "reclassifications," which, although not listed as a separate element, does not fit the definition of any of the other elements. It also subdivides the "net assets" element and the related components of income into three "classes," which presumably are something other than elements although their nature is undefined. All this vagueness and confusion has made the conceptual framework a monstrosity.

Contributions. The explanation for these new terms can be traced to the issue of contributions – specifically, those contributions received in one accounting period whose use is restricted to a later period. In a business, magazine subscriptions and similar prepayments are held as liabilities until the period to which they relate, when they become revenues. In a nonprofit organization, restricted operating contributions essentially have the same nature. The FASB, however, decided that, unlike magazine subscriptions, such contributions did not fit the definition of liabilities because the donor might not demand the return of the contribution if it were not used in the later period. To most people, this is a distinction without a difference. Nevertheless, after much discussion, the board decided to make contributions a new element for nonprofits, to be treated as revenues in the year of receipt.

Many respondents to the exposure draft strongly criticized this idea, pointing out that it did not match revenues with the expenses incurred in the later period for the restricted purpose. Even more important, the proposed element failed to distinguish between two fundamentally different types of contributions: those related to operating activities, such as annual gifts and contributions for restricted operating purposes, and those for endowment and similar capital purposes, whose income was available for operations but whose corpus had to be kept intact.

The final version of the statement, a compromise, eliminates the separate element for contributions. Instead, the FASB divides net assets (that is, equity) and changes in net assets (that is, income) into three classes: (1) unrestricted, which includes the usual types of revenues plus unrestricted contributions; (2) temporarily restricted, which includes contributions received in one period for use in a later period; and (3) permanently restricted, which includes endowment.

As with many compromises, the result makes no sense. Of its several absurdities, the worst is that although the statement divides net assets into three classes, it lumps all the entity's assets together. This is despite the fact that the laws of all 50 states require nonprofit organizations to separate endowment assets from operating assets. Such a separation is, in any case, obviously essential in judging an organization's ability to meet its operating financial needs.

Recognition & measurement

From the outset of the concepts project, the board deferred the resolution of tough issues. It justified the deferrals by maintaining that these issues related to "recognition and measurement," the subject of a later statement.

The result was Statement No. 5, issued in December 1984, which became a catchall for unresolved issues. In tackling these issues, some of the board members became more set in their opinions. To get something out, they had to make all sorts of compromises. Moreover, the definitions given in Statement No. 3 limited their ability to address the recognition and measurement issues sensibly. Because of this, Statement No. 5 is seriously flawed and raises more questions than it answers.

The purpose of a concepts statement is to assess what financial reporting should be, not to describe what current practices are. Statement No. 5, however, deals primarily with the board's perception of current practices, with no guidelines for improvement.

FASB concepts

The FASB conceptual framework consists of six statements of financial concepts, which, except for one dissent in Statement No. 5, were adopted unanimously. Issued from 1978 to 1985, they are outlined as follows:

Statement No. 1, *Objectives of Financial Reporting for Business Enterprises*, issued in November 1978, describes accounting's environment and the presumed needs of users of accounting information in more than half of its 56 paragraphs. Only a few paragraphs discuss accounting concepts as such.

Statement No. 2, *Qualitative Characteristics of Accounting Information*, issued in May 1980, describes criteria that are relevant in deciding on accounting standards and their application to specific events in 144 paragraphs.

Statement No. 3, *Elements of Financial Statements of Business Enterprises*, issued in December 1980, purports to define ten basic elements in 89 paragraphs, but six of the elements are derived arithmetically from two others.

Statement No. 4, *Objectives of Financial Reporting by Nonbusiness Organizations*, issued in December 1980, was presumably intended to expand Statement No. 1 to incorporate the objectives of nonbusiness enterprises that differ from those described in the earlier statement, but it is as long as Statement No. 1.

Statement No. 5, *Recognition and Measurement in Financial Statements of Business Enterprises*, issued in December 1984, summarizes current practices in its 91 paragraphs rather than making a statement of what the concepts should be.

Statement No. 6, *Elements of Financial Statements*, issued in December 1985, repeats, and therefore replaces, the paragraphs in Statement No. 3 about business enterprises and adds about 40 paragraphs on nonbusiness enterprises. It also states that Statement No. 2, without change, applies to nonprofit organizations.

This is no way to resolve issues, unless you accept the premise that accounting standards are already perfect.

The statement does say in several places that the concepts are subject to "gradual change or evolution," but it gives no indication of the desirable direction. The FASB can thus use Statement No. 5 to support *any* future standard, as long as it isn't revolutionary. In some disciplines, an occasional conceptual revolution is the most important way of making progress.

Statement No. 5 also presents concepts without clarifying them. In one place it says that revenues are "sometimes recognized before sale if readily realizable." Surely the board doesn't mean to imply that a company should report revenues from products as soon as they are produced – even if they haven't been shipped – as long as they are produced under valid contracts or have a known market. But that is how the statement reads.

Accounting is a measurement system that uses the arithmetic operations of addition and subtraction. You add individual asset items to obtain totals for classes of assets and total assets, and subtract expenses from revenues to arrive at net income. It is a simple fact that numbers cannot be added or subtracted unless they have the same attribute. To put it another way, you can't add apples and oranges – but if you call them "pieces of fruit," or if you express both apples and oranges in terms of their cost or some other attribute, then you can add the resulting numbers.

Statement No. 5 disregards this basic fact about measurement systems. Instead of settling on a single attribute, it discusses five of them – historical cost, current cost, current market value, net realizable value, and present value – and says that each has particular cases for which it is appropriate. The single attribute that is necessary to make sense of the additions and subtractions used in accounting does exist; otherwise accounting numbers would be a meaningless mishmash. The attribute is "financial resources" – the flow of financial resources into, through, and out of the entity, and the status of these resources as of a particular moment.

Criteria

The principal area in which FASB does good work is with respect to criteria. In Statement No. 2, which is by far the best of the six, the board recommends criteria for evaluating alternative proposals for standards and practice. The statement defines the essential characteristics of accounting information as relevance (the information should help decision makers make decisions) and reliability (the information should be reasonably objective and error free and should represent what it purports to represent).

These qualities are not new. What is new, and important, is the statement that "reliability and relevance often impinge on each other." The trade-off between relevance and reliability and the relative weights assigned to each is at the heart of many disagreements over accounting standards. Certain types of stock options, for example, represent an expense at the time they are granted, and the amount is relevant information. The decision about whether to recognize this expense turns on a judgment as to whether a sufficiently reliable approximation of the amount can be made.

To the two dominant characteristics of relevance and reliability, Statement No. 2 adds benefit and cost: accounting should provide information that is worth more than its cost. An obvious point, but one that is sometimes overlooked by advocates of certain esoteric practices.

Causes of failure

Developing a conceptual framework for financial accounting is not easy. The FASB's predecessors, the Committee on Accounting Procedures and the Accounting Principles Board, considered several proposals but accepted none.

Part of the trouble is the theoretical nature of the job. Many disciplines recognize the distinction between theory and practice; medicine, for instance, generally acknowledges the difference between a practicing physician and a theoretical biochemist. No one expects a physician to make breakthroughs in biochemistry, and no one expects a biochemist to heal patients.

In accounting the distinction is not as clear. Most accountants are practitioners, as preparers of accounting information, auditors, or teachers. Only a handful are interested in making a career as theorists, and for those few the opportunities are limited to the largest public accounting and investment firms and a few university positions. Excellent accountants may be interested in theory as an avocation, especially after retirement, but they have no good way of disseminating their views. Moreover, accounting requires a special kind of theorist: a person who has a thorough knowledge of both the real world and accounting concepts.

The Business Roundtable, the president of General Motors, the Financial Executives Institute, and many others have been vocal in their opinion that the members of the Financial Accounting Standards Board should be "practical." They should indeed be practical – in the sense that they understand what the world is really like – but they must also be theoreticians.

The FASB has an almost insurmountable problem in identifying and attracting qualified conceptualizers to its staff. It cannot match the compensation of public accounting firms. It cannot offer the status or tenure of a university appointment. It cannot hold out the prospect of public recognition that comes from published articles – at least, it has not done so.

There are only a few fundamental issues in financial accounting: the asset and liability versus the revenue and expense approach, the historical exchange-value versus the inflation-adjusted approach, the proprietary versus the entity theory, and the question of which attribute accounting should measure. Unless a concepts project resolves these issues at the outset, the subsequent debate over a framework will be interminable and the resulting statements inconsistent. The FASB did not resolve the first three issues until Statement No. 5, and even there it equivocated; it has not addressed the attribute question at all.

Part of the difficulty can be attributed to the number of distractions that diverted the attention of the concepts staff. The 1977 hearings before the Senate Subcommittee on Reports, Accounting and Management (the Metcalf hearings) took much time. The experiment with supplementary price-level-adjusted financial statements consumed a great many man-days in what was, in retrospect, a relatively unproductive effort. In one year alone, board and staff members gave 300 speeches.

Poor presentation

Part of the board's difficulty in giving clear answers to accounting questions is its long-winded presentation. A set of concepts should be short; its text should consist of the concepts with examples and explanatory material, but no more. The FASB statements introduce a great deal of unnecessary material, which serves only to obscure the issues. The 1976 draft on objectives, for example, has three paragraphs on objectives and just over three pages of explanatory material. The next year's draft on the same topic is about twice as long. And the final statement is five times longer than the original. I submit that the board could have stated the objectives in six paragraphs or less.

Granted that the need for a balance sheet and funds-flow statement should be mentioned and that the sentence about financial statements being pitched at the level of the knowledgeable reader is important, but is there any point in explaining that "the United States has a highly developed economy" with several long paragraphs that might have been taken from a high school social studies text? Such material is not only unnecessary but it can also be misleading. Although the statement focuses on earnings, for example, it speaks favorably in a number of places about cash flows. This ambiguity has led many people to infer erroneously that the board wants to shift accounting from an accrual to a cash basis.

Another problem with the board's framework is that it doesn't provide a firm foundation on which to build individual standards. Statutes and court opinions make innumerable references to the Constitution of the United States; this is only natural, since the Constitution was designed to guide the drafting of laws. By contrast, the pronouncements of the Financial Accounting Standards Board make few references to the concepts statements that should be guiding its decisions. The board's nonuse of its own material is perhaps the best indication that the material is unsatisfactory.

Between April 1979 and December 1985, for example, the FASB issued 63 statements and 44 interpretations and technical bulletins—a total of 107 pronouncements, containing several thousand paragraphs. A search by the National Automated Accounting Research System turned up only 28 references to concepts statements in these thousands of paragraphs. It might be argued that the concepts statements guided the thinking of board members, even though this was not made explicit. One has to strain, though, to find indications of this in the text or even in the sections labeled "basis for conclusions."

The lack of guidance provided by the concepts statements may help explain why, in its 13 years of existence, the board has not tackled some of accounting's basic problems. An organization can still choose either of two completely inconsistent inventory methods. It is free to use any depreciation method that is "rational." The 88 standards published through 1985 address only about a dozen broad accounting issues, as contrasted with the multitude of fire-fighting topics like "Accounting for Tax Benefits Related to U.K. Tax Legislation Concerning Stock Relief." The two-paragraph treatment of expenses in Statement No. 5 is grossly superficial, and the related topic of the meaning of "cost" is dealt with only in a footnote. There are only vague references as to which types of gains or losses should be recognized in a given period.

New approach

The millions of dollars invested in the FASB's conceptual framework project may not have been entirely wasted. An analysis of the results suggests the outline of an acceptable framework, and a close look at the weaknesses in the former approach reveals a better way to proceed.

These are the major points I think a conceptual framework for accounting should include:

1   The framework should be limited to the information in the primary financial statements. (Broadening it to include supplementary information leads to an undesirable dilution of effort, as was demonstrated by the inflation accounting program.)
2   The objective of financial statements should be to provide useful information about an entity for those who make decisions based on such information. (As was demonstrated in Statements No. 1 and No. 4, an attempt to make an exhaustive list of users and their needs serves no important purpose.)

3   Standards governing the information in financial statements should be based on an appropriate trade-off between relevance and reliability. (This is a message from Statement No. 2.)

4   Financial statements should summarize the economic performance and status of an entity as a consequence of events that have occurred during an accounting period. (This idea permeates all the statements.)

5   Financial accounting should focus primarily on reporting an entity's performance in maintaining its financial capital during an accounting period, as measured by its net income.

6   The effect of highly unusual events – whose inclusion would result in a serious distortion of reported performance – should be excluded from net income and entered directly in entity equity. (A standard should spell out the nature of these exceptional events. This is consistent with present practice.)

7   Net income should be measured as the difference between the revenues and the expenses of a period.

8   Revenues are additions to entity equity resulting from events of the period, including realized gains. (This general statement needs to be made more specific in a standard that describes when revenues should be recognized and how the amounts are to be measured.)

9   Expenses are costs incurred in a current or previous period that will not benefit future periods, as well as reasonably possible losses that are identified in the current period. (A standard should make this more specific and include a statement that the costs of using capital, including equity capital, are included as expenses. Unless revenues are at least equal to expenses, including these costs, the entity has not maintained its financial capital.)

10   The balance sheet should report the sources of an entity's financial capital and the forms in which that capital existed as of the balance sheet date. (This statement is probably the most significant departure from the material in the concepts statements. This concept, however, fits the meaning of the balance sheet in current practice better than the meaning suggested by the concepts statements.)

11   An entity's sources of capital are liabilities, shareholder equity, contributed equity, and entity equity. (A standard should define these elements thus: liabilities are amounts owed to nonowner parties; shareholder equity is the amount of capital contributed by shareholders, either directly or because a portion of equity interest has not yet been paid to them;

contributed equity is donated capital, usually in nonprofit organizations; and entity equity is the capital that an entity has generated, as measured by its cumulative net income.)

12   Assets are the forms in which the entity's capital exist as of the balance sheet date. They consist of monetary amounts controlled by the entity and costs that will become expenses in later periods. (Standards should describe the recognition and measurement of assets. Basically, monetary assets, with the possible exception of investments, should be measured at the present value of the amount likely to be received; other assets should be measured at unamortized cost.)

13   Accounting should report the flow of financial resources into, through, and out of the organization, measured in monetary amounts unadjusted for changes in price levels. (This statement specifies the attribute that is the basis of accounting measurement.)[1]

Note that this list does not mention cash flows. I see no need to discuss cash flows in a concepts statement (except to say that financial accounting does not focus on cash flows).

There is one, and only one, basic difference between the concepts outlined above and present practice: the treatment of capital furnished by shareholders. If shareholders are regarded as merely one source of capital, the amount of capital furnished by shareholders should be recorded separately from capital generated by the entity itself. The use of shareholder capital has a cost to the entity. Although this concept is new to accounting, economists have almost universally accepted it.

Implementing change

Given that change is needed in articulating a guideline for accounting, how can this be accomplished? It makes sense for a private-sector body, rather than a government agency, to develop a conceptual framework and set standards for financial accounting. The Financial Accounting Standards Board is well established and has the support of both the public and private sectors. There is no reason to expect that a different body would do a better job. On the other hand, the FASB developed and blessed the six concepts statements, and it is unreasonable to expect the board to disavow them now.

A politically acceptable solution would be for the board to develop an alternative conceptual framework with a different name, perhaps "guidelines." The board could simply let the six existing concepts statements fade away, emphasizing that they are not authoritative (which the board already suggests in the introduction to each of them).

1 For a more complete outline, see my book, *Tell It Like It Was* (Homewood, Ill.: Richard D. Irwin, 1983).

The FASB could expose these guidelines for public discussion, while making it clear that their primary use is to help the board in developing standards. They should cover the topics listed in the preceding section and be not much longer than that list.

The set of guidelines should be adopted as a whole. If accepted piecemeal, the final package is likely to be internally inconsistent. When disagreements surface, alternative guidelines should be prepared and their internal consistency, as well as their consistency with the real world, should be analyzed. This should always be done in the context of a single set of guidelines.

The board should then develop clear, consistent standards on the necessary topics: the concept of cost; the recognition and measurement of revenues (including gains); the recognition and measurement of expenses (including losses); the treatment of contributed capital and other changes in equity that do not flow through income; and the recognition and measurement of monetary amounts on the balance sheet. As FASB standards, these would automatically become generally accepted accounting principles. The board should strengthen the principles' status by referring to them in each of the conventional standards developed.

The board's director of research should seek the best people in the country and contract with them to develop drafts of these standards. One person should develop each draft with the advice of a task force, as a committee is unlikely to agree often enough to produce good work. A board member should act as a mentor to each contractor, suggesting what probably would or wouldn't be acceptable to the board. Contractors should be assured that their output will be discussed by the board and that they will have an opportunity to defend their work.

Relying on outside contractors to develop drafts of standards would be an unusual step for the FASB. It is, however, a logical way to proceed. And it seems to work well for other standard-setting bodies.

Financial accounting desperately needs an authoritative conceptual framework. Without it, standard setters will continue to approach each issue on an ad hoc basis and argue from their own premises and concepts, which are not made explicit. The result is that the FASB takes years to develop standards, which are sometimes inconsistent. Moreover, practitioners have no common point of departure to decide on how to account for events that are not specifically covered by accounting standards.

While the FASB's 12-year, multimillion-dollar effort to develop a framework has failed, it has suggested valuable lessons on how to succeed the next time around. Although the frustrations from the previous effort make members reluctant to start over, the FASB should not give up. The goal is within reach, and the board should make a determined effort to reach it. ▽

Reprint 87103

Efforts to revitalize manufacturing industries cannot succeed if outdated accounting and control systems remain unchanged

Yesterday's accounting undermines production

Robert S. Kaplan

Many U.S. companies are now exploiting new process technologies, new inventory and materials handling systems, new computer-based abilities in design, engineering, and production, and new approaches to work force management. But these developments, promising as they are, rest on a foundation that is obsolete and in need of repair.

As the author makes clear, most accounting and control systems have major problems: they distort product costs; they do not produce the key nonfinancial data required for effective and efficient operations; and the data they do produce reflect external reporting requirements far more than they do the reality of the new manufacturing environment. Only when management accounting systems are brought in line with the new competitive environment will efforts to upgrade production prove genuinely successful – and permanent.

Mr. Kaplan, formerly dean of the business school at Carnegie-Mellon University, holds a joint appointment as professor of industrial administration at Carnegie-Mellon University and as the Arthur Lowes Dickenson Professor of Accounting at the Harvard Business School. This article grows out of his research on the new challenges for accounting systems in manufacturing industries.

Illustrations by John Devaney.

The present era of intense global competition is leading U.S. companies toward a renewed commitment to excellence in manufacturing. Attention to the quality of products and processes, the level of inventories, and the improvement of work-force policies has made manufacturing once again a key element in the strategies of companies intending to be world-class competitors. There remains, however, a major – and largely unnoticed – obstacle to the lasting success of this revolution in the organization and technology of manufacturing operations. Most companies still use the same cost accounting and management control systems that were developed decades ago for a competitive environment drastically different from that of today. Consider, for example, the following cases drawn from actual company experiences.

During Richard Thompson's two years as manager of the Industrial Products Division of the Acme Corporation, the division enjoyed such greatly improved profitability that he was promoted to more senior corporate responsibility. Thompson's replacement, however, found the division's manufacturing capability greatly eroded and a plunge in profitability inevitable.

Careful analysis of operations during Thompson's tenure revealed that:

☐ Increased profitability had been largely caused by an unexpected jump in demand that permitted the division's facilities to operate near capacity.

☐ Despite this expansion, the division's market share had decreased.

☐ Costs had been reduced by not maintaining equipment, by operating it beyond rated capacity, by not investing in new equipment or product development, and by imposing stress on workers to the point of alienating them.

☐   Many costs had been absorbed into a bloated inventory position.

☐   Unit productivity had actually fallen.

By this time, however, Thompson was secure in his senior position and was still receiving credit for the high profits Industrial Products had earned under his direction.

The Carmel Corporation had made significant investments in labor-saving equipment. Yet with total costs, particularly overhead, still increasing, it was hard pressed to maintain market share with prices that fully recovered all of its costs. Carmel used a standard cost accounting system that allocated all nondirect costs on the basis of direct labor hours. The company had installed this procedure many years ago when direct labor accounted for more than 60% of total costs and machinery was both simple and inexpensive. Over the years, however, investment in sophisticated new machinery had greatly reduced the direct labor content of the company's products.

Staff costs rose as Carmel expanded its design and engineering staffs to develop specialized high-margin products. Because these new products required advanced materials, Carmel also expanded its purchase of semifinished components from suppliers. With direct labor (at an average wage of $12 per hour) plunging as a fraction of total costs, the accounting system was allocating the growing capital and overhead costs to a shrinking pool of direct labor hours.

The predictable result: a total cost per direct labor hour in excess of $60 – and projections that it would soon rise to $80. Worse, efforts to offset these higher hourly rates by substituting capital and purchased materials for in-house production only compounded the problem. The accounting system was distracting management attention from the expansion of indirect costs.

Both these examples offer a pointed reminder that poorly designed or outdated accounting and control systems can distort the realities of manufacturing performance. Equally important, such systems can place out of reach most of the promised benefits from new CIM (computer-integrated manufacturing) processes. As information workers like design engineers and systems analysts replace traditional blue-collar workers in factories, accounting conventions that allocate overhead to direct labor hours will be at best irrelevant and more likely counterproductive to a company's manufacturing operations. And with the new manufacturing technology now available, variable costs will disappear except for purchases of materials and the energy required to operate equipment.

Not only will labor costs be mostly fixed; many of them will become sunk costs. The investment in software to operate and maintain computer-based manufacturing equipment must take place before any production starts, and of course that investment will be independent of the number of items produced using the software program. With the decreasing importance of variable labor costs, companies that allocate the fixed, sunk costs of equipment and information systems according to anticipated production volumes will distort the underlying economics of the new manufacturing environment.

In this environment, companies will need to concentrate on obtaining maximum effectiveness from their equipment and from their increasing investment in information workers and in what they produce. Controlling variable labor costs will become a lower priority. This major change in emphasis requires that managers learn new ways to think about and measure both product costs and product profitability.

Nonfinancial aspects of manufacturing performance

It is unlikely, however, that any cost accounting system can adequately summarize a company's manufacturing operations. Today's accounting systems evolved from the scientific management movement in the early part of the twentieth century. They were instrumental in promoting the efficiency of mass production enterprises, particularly those producing relatively few standard products with a high direct labor content. Reliance on these systems in today's competitive environment, which is characterized by products with much lower direct labor content, will provide an inadequate picture of manufacturing efficiency and effectiveness.

Measurement systems for today's manufacturing operations must consider:

Quality. To excel as a world-class manufacturer, a company must be totally committed to quality – that is, each component, subassembly, and finished good should be produced in conformity to specifications. Such a commitment to quality entails

1 See, for example, Jinichiro Nakane and Robert W. Hall, "Management Specs for Stockless Production," HBR May-June 1983, p. 84; Larry P. Ritzman, Barry E. King, and Lee J. Krajewski, "Manufacturing Performance – Pulling the Right Levers," HBR March-April 1984, p. 143; and Hal F. Mather, "The Case for Skimpy Inventories," HBR January-February 1984, p. 40.

major changes in the way companies design products, work with suppliers, train employees, and operate and maintain equipment. But this commitment must also extend to a company's measurement systems. Data on the percentage of defects, frequency of breakdowns, percentage of finished goods completed without any rework required, and on the incidence and frequency of defects discovered by customers should be a vital part of any company's quality-enhancement program. Otherwise, the impact of variations in quality will show up in cost and market share data too late and at too aggregate a level to be of help to management. Direct quality indicators should be reported frequently at all levels of a manufacturing organization.

Inventory. A second nonfinancial indicator of manufacturing performance is inventory. American managers are well versed in optimizing inventory levels according to the economic order quantity (EOQ) model, which balances the cost of additional setup time with the cost of carrying inventory. They are less familiar with the effort, common among Japanese producers, to eliminate setup times and to implement just-in-time inventory control systems, which together reduce drastically overall levels of work-in-process (WIP) inventory.[1]

Many of the savings in reduced working capital, factory storage, and materials handling from cutting WIP will eventually be reflected in lower total manufacturing costs. But many of the savings that arise from transactions *not* taken—less borrowing to finance inventory, for example, or less need to expand factory floor space—will not be reflected in these costs. Therefore, such direct measures as average batch sizes, WIP, and inventory of purchased items will provide much more accurate and timely information on a company's manufacturing performance than will the behavior of average manufacturing costs.

Productivity. Direct measures of productivity are a third important set of nonfinancial indicators. Even in companies publicly committed to productivity improvements, accurate measurement of productivity is often impossible because accounting systems are designed to capture dollar-based transactions only. Without precise data on units produced, labor hours used, materials processed, energy consumed, and capital employed, administrators must deflate dollar amounts by aggregate price indices to obtain approximate physical measures of productivity. But errors in approximation often arise that can easily mask any period-to-period changes in real productivity.

Alternatively, managers rely on partial productivity measures, such as value added per employee or output per direct labor hour, which attribute all productivity changes to labor. These mea-

sures tend to overlook gains from the more efficient use of capital, energy, and managerial effort and so encourage the substitution of capital, indirect labor, energy, and processed materials for direct labor. But as direct labor costs decline relative to total manufacturing costs, it becomes more–not less–important to focus on total factor productivity.

Nor can managers finesse these measurement problems by looking only at aggregate data on profitability. In the short run, product profitability may be caused more by relative price changes and holding gains not recognized by historical cost-based systems than by structural improvements in the production process. A temporary expansion of demand can, for example, enable a company to boost its prices faster than its growth in costs. In the long run, however, the higher wages paid by U.S. companies will lead to competitive difficulties–unless offset by higher productivity. During the 1960s and 1970s, many U.S. companies earned a comfortable profit and did not notice that their productivity had begun to stagnate or even decline. They are noticing now.

Innovation. Some companies choose to compete not by efficiently producing mature products that have general customer acceptance and stable designs but by introducing a constant stream of new products. Customers buy the products of these innovative companies because of the value of their unique characteristics, not because the products are cheaper than those of competitors. For innovating companies, the key to success is high performance products, timely delivery, and product customization. Attempts to impose cost minimization and efficiency criteria–especially early in the product development process–will be counterproductive.

Cost accounting systems, however, rarely distinguish between products that compete on the basis of cost and those that compete on the basis of unique characteristics valued by purchasers. Thus, it is difficult to manufacture new products in facilities that also manufacture mature products since plant managers, evaluated by an accounting system that stresses efficiency and productivity, find it disruptive to make products for which both the designs and the process technology are still evolving. Companies that cannot afford the luxury of a separate facility for new product manufacturing must learn to de-emphasize traditional cost measurements during the start-up phase of new products and to monitor directly their performance, quality, and timely delivery.

Work force. Another limitation of traditional cost accounting systems is their inability to measure the skills, training, and morale of the work force. As much recent experience attests, if employees do not share a company's goals, the company cannot survive as a first-rate competitor. Hence, the morale, attitudes, skill, and education of employees can be as valuable to a company as its tangible assets.

Some companies, noting the importance of their human resources, conduct periodic surveys of employee attitudes and morale. They also monitor educational and skill levels, promotion and training, and the absenteeism and turnover of people under each manager's supervision. These people-based measures are weighted heavily when managers' performance is evaluated. Meeting profit or cost budgets does not lead to a positive job rating if it is accompanied by any deterioration in these people-based measures.

In summary, the financial measures generated by traditional cost accounting systems provide an inadequate summary of a company's manufacturing operations. Today's global competition requires that nonfinancial measures–on quality, inventory levels, productivity, flexibility, deliverability, and employees–also be used in the evaluation of a company's manufacturing performance. Companies that achieve satisfactory financial performance but show stagnant or deteriorating performance on nonfinancial indicators are unlikely to become–or long remain–world-class competitors.

Improving control systems

Improving manufacturing performance requires more of accounting systems than the timely provision of relevant financial and nonfinancial data. Fundamental changes in management control systems are also needed. In particular, there is a need to rethink the way companies use summary financial measures like ROI to coordinate, motivate, and evaluate their decentralized operating units.

The ROI measure was developed earlier in this century to help in the management of the new multi-activity corporations that were then forming. ROI was used as an indicator of the efficiency of diverse operating departments, as a means for evaluating requests for new capital investment, and as an overall measure of the financial performance of the entire company.

Through the use of ROI control, early twentieth century corporations achieved a specialization of managerial talent. Managers of functional departments (manufacturing, sales, finance, and purchasing) could become specialists and pursue strategies for their departments that increased the ROI of the entire company. Senior managers, freed from day-

DEVANEY

to-day operating responsibility, could focus on coordinating the company's diverse activities and developing its long-term strategies.

In practice, decentralization via ROI control permitted senior executives to be physically and organizationally separated from their manufacturing operations. For many years, this separation was a valuable and necessary feature that enabled corporations to expand into many diverse lines of business. Recently, however, problems with running corporations "by the numbers"—that is, with excessive reliance on ROI measures but without detailed knowledge of divisions' operations and technology—have become uncomfortably apparent.

Inflation & ROI

The financial executives who pioneered in the application of ROI measures were not concerned with the distortions introduced by inflation. After World War II, however, as ROI-based control systems came into widespread use, continuous price increases gave a steady upward bias to ROI.

When fixed assets and inventory are not restated for price level changes after acquisition, net income is overstated and investment is understated. Thus managers who retain older, mostly depreciated assets report much higher ROIs than managers who invest in new assets. Such apparent differences in profitability, of course, have nothing to do with actual differences in the rates of return of the two classes of assets.

Financial accounting mentality

Such distortions of economic performance are but one manifestation of a broader problem: the use in a company's internal reporting and evaluation systems of accounting practices and conventions developed for external reporting. This is, for the most part, a recent phenomenon and is more common in the United States than in other parts of the world.

In Europe, many companies have one department to collect and analyze data for internal operations and another to prepare external reports. Some companies, like Philips in the Netherlands, even report to stockholders on the basis used to evaluate internal operations. By contrast, contemporary practice in the United States is to use for internal purposes conventions either developed for external reporting or mandated by such external reporting authorities as the Financial Accounting Standards Board and the SEC.

Interest expense

For example, many American corporations regularly allocate corporate expenses – say, interest costs – to divisions and profit centers according to some arbitrary measure of a unit's assets or working capital. Now, it is sensible to charge divisions for capital employed. It is not sensible, however, to use a pro rata share of the interest expense reported on external financial statements as the appropriate internal cost of capital. Such a procedure implies that a company financed entirely through equity would allocate no capital charges to divisions since it has no recorded interest expense.

Consider, at the other extreme, an autonomous division engaged in real estate whose assets are mostly debt financed. The financial accounting mentality would have this division bear a higher interest charge against earnings than would divisions financed more heavily by equity. But does anyone believe that the cost of debt capital is higher than that of equity capital?

Divisions should be charged for their investment in net controllable assets through a divisional cost of capital, perhaps adjusted to allow lower charges for working capital than for higher-risk fixed assets. Few companies use such a method today, perhaps because the divisional capital charges will "over-absorb" a company's actual interest expense. But considering actual interest expense as a company's only cost of invested capital is more a limitation of contemporary financial reporting than it is a criticism of charging divisions for the full cost of their investments.

Pension costs

Financial accounting practices can also lead to bad cost accounting in the allocation of pension costs. For example, prior service costs are sunk costs. They represent an obligation of a company for the past service of its employees. No current or future action of the company can affect this obligation. The amortization of prior service costs must, however, be recognized as a current expense in the company's financial statements. Therefore, many companies allocate prior service costs to divisions.

One company allocated these costs in proportion to pension benefits accrued. A plant with an older work force received almost all of its division's prior service costs, but several newer plants with much younger workers bore almost none. This arbitrary allocation produced a $4 per labor hour cost penalty on the older plant. As a result, the company was shifting work from the older plant to the newer ones. In addition, the older plant was losing market share as it raised prices in an attempt to earn a satisfactory margin over its high labor costs. Put simply, the company became a victim of its financial accounting mentality: first it allocated a noncontrollable, sunk cost to its plants and then it relied on this arbitrarily allocated cost for pricing and product sourcing decisions.

Other distortions

Distortions created by the financial accounting mentality intrude on many other internal measurements. How often, for instance, do executives, when measuring a division's investment base for an ROI calculation, include leased assets only when, according to FASB regulations, they must be capitalized on the external financial statements? Are development and start-up expenses, including software development, considered part of the investment in a computer-integrated manufacturing process, or are these investments in intangibles expensed as incurred because, according to SFAS 2, this treatment is mandated for external reporting? Do companies translate operations in foreign countries according to their economic exposure overseas, or do they use whatever translation method the FASB happens to be mandating at the time?

The point, of course, is that companies seeking to compete effectively must devise cost accounting systems that reflect their investment decisions and cost structures. Internal accounting practices should be driven by corporate strategy, not by FASB and SEC requirements for external reporting. Surely, the cost of record keeping in an electronic age is sufficiently low that aggregating transaction data differently for external and internal purposes cannot be a burdensome task.

Financial entrepreneurship

Another set of difficulties with ROI-based measurements stems from the ability of executives to generate greater profits from financial activities than from managing their assets better. Sixty years ago managers knew that higher profits and ROI came from efficient production, aggressive marketing, and a continual flow of product and process improvements. During the past 20 years, however, as it has become more difficult to increase profits through selling, production, and R&D, some companies have looked to accounting and financial activities to generate earnings.

At first, these activities – switching from accelerated to straight-line depreciation, for example – did little harm. Occasionally they proved costly, as when companies opted to pay unnecessary taxes by delaying or refusing a switch to LIFO because of its adverse impact on reported profits. Today, however, the romance with these devices is in full swing: mergers and acquisitions, divestitures and spinoffs, debt swaps and discounted debt repurchases, debt defeasance, sale-leaseback arrangements, and leveraged buyouts.

Some of these activities may create value for shareholders (current research is still attempting to sort out the net effect of these financial activities). Still, it is hard to imagine that a focus on creating wealth through the rearrangement of ownership claims rather than on managing tangible and intangible assets more effectively will help companies survive as world-class competitors. Ultimately, wealth must be created by the imaginative and intelligent management of assets, not by devising novel financing and ownership arrangements for those assets.

Intangible assets

The final and most damaging problem with ROI-based measures is the incentive they give managers to reduce expenditures on discretionary and intangible investments. When sluggish sales or growing costs make profit targets hard to achieve, managers often try to prop up short-term earnings by cutting expenditures on R&D, promotion, distribution, quality improvement, applications engineering, human resources, and customer relations—all of which are, of course, vital to a company's long-term performance. The immediate effect of such reductions is to boost reported profitability—but at the risk of sacrificing the company's competitive position.

The opportunity for a company to increase reported income by forgoing intangible investments illustrates a fundamental flaw in the financial accounting model. This flaw compromises the role of short-term profits as a valid and reliable indicator of a company's economic health. A company's economic value is not merely the sum of the values of its tangible assets, whether measured at historic cost, replacement cost, or current market prices. It also includes the value of intangible assets: its stock of products and processes, employee talent and morale, customer loyalty, reliable suppliers, efficient distribution network, and the like.

Suppose this stock of intangible assets could be valued each period. Then, when the company decreased its expenditures on these assets, their subsequent decline in value would lower the company's reported income. We do not, however, have methods to value objectively intangible assets. Therefore, reported earnings cannot show a company's decline in value when it depletes its stock of intangible assets. It is this defect in the financial accounting model that makes the quarterly or annual income number an inadequate summary of the change in value of the company during the period.

The task at hand

Present cost accounting and management control systems rest on concepts developed almost a century ago when the nature of competition and the demands for internal information were very different from what they are today. When companies now make arbitrary allocations of corporate expenses to divisions and products, accounting systems may provide even less valid cost data than did the cost accumulation systems in use 50 years ago. In general, though, an accounting model derived for the efficient production of a few standardized products with high direct labor content will not be appropriate for an automated production environment where the factors critical to success are quality, flexibility, and the efficient use of expensive information workers and capital.

General managers must be alert to the inadequacies of their present measurement systems. It is doubtful whether any company can be successfully run by the numbers, but certainly the numbers being generated by today's systems provide little basis for managerial decisions and control. Managers require both improved financial numbers and nonfinancial indicators of manufacturing performance. Because no measurement system, however well designed, can capture all the relevant information, any operational system must be supplemented by direct observation in the field. The separation of senior management from operations that the ROI formula made possible 80 years ago will have to be partially repealed. Successful senior managers must be knowledgeable about the current organization and technology of their operations.

For their part, accounting and financial executives must redirect their energies—and their thinking—from external reporting to the more effective management of their companies' tangible and intangible assets. Internal management accounting systems need renovation. Yesterday's internal costing and control practices cannot be allowed to exist in isolation from a company's manufacturing environment—not, that is, if the company wishes to flourish as a world-class competitor. ▽

Reprint 84406

*Doctor, lawyer, industry chief—
they all have
different needs*

What kind of
cost system
do you need?

Michael J. Sandretto

Although cost accounting is conceptually simple, it is not an all-purpose management tool. In some situations where a detailed cost system would be desirable, the expense of designing, installing, and operating it is too high; in other situations where detailed information is readily obtainable, it has little value.

Many managers, failing to recognize the relationship between cost accounting and environment, spend hundreds of thousands of dollars on systems that do not suit their production processes. Fortunately, new computer systems have enlarged the options. This author shows how managers can choose a system that works well for their purposes, providing both good control and effective analysis. He also describes the situations where cost control and cost analysis are likely to be crucial to an organization.

Mr. Sandretto is assistant professor of business administration at the Harvard Business School, where he teaches management control and cost accounting in the MBA program. He was formerly corporate controller of Knowles Electronics, a Chicago-based manufacturer, and is the author, with Cornelius J. Casey, of an HBR article, "Internal Uses of Accounting for Inflation" November-December 1981.

"Our cost system is state of the art. It provides actual and standard costs for each product we make. We can calculate variance from standard on a daily basis by product, by employee, and by machine. We use costs for pricing on a weekly or even a daily basis. Our entire strategy is based on our cost system." (President, Ajax Manufacturing)

"We've had four controllers in seven years. Three consultants have tried to install a cost system, but annual errors in our inventory still average 10%. I doubt if any cost figure I'm shown is within 10% of its real cost unless it's by accident. Cost accounting is a huge waste of money; I don't know why we even bother." (President, Bee Company)

From these statements it might appear that Ajax has an exceptional controller while the president of Bee Company is an unusually poor judge of both controllers and consultants. A careful review of the situations of these hypothetical companies, however, would almost certainly lead to a different conclusion. For if Bee Company's controllers or consultants had worked for Ajax, the result would probably have been considered a state-of-the-art cost system. And had the person who designed Ajax's system worked for Bee Company, the outcome would likely have been a cost system that the president considered marginally acceptable.

Managers involved in a job-order manufacturing process like the one at Ajax most often have highly positive opinions of cost accounting while managers in complex assembly manufacturing operations like those of Bee Company often hold negative views.

The feasibility of a particular cost system and its usefulness to a manager depend on many different factors. In some situations a detailed cost system is desirable, and the expense of designing, installing, and operating it is low. In other cases, although cost information would be of value, obtaining it is too expensive. Elsewhere, even detailed cost information has limited value.

Unfortunately, many managers fail to recognize that numerous factors influence cost accounting, including production method, product type, corporate strategy, and market conditions. Some companies spend several hundred thousand dollars for cost systems that are never implemented because the systems do not suit the production process, and the managers responsible have lost their jobs.

Nonetheless, because of the recent availability of computer software that can produce accurate and detailed information on basic operations, many managers are renewing their efforts in cost accounting. In addition, with direct costs now constituting a smaller share of total cost, it is more important to separate costs into their fixed and variable elements and to allocate fixed costs in greater detail. This is especially true where costs are crucial for pricing.

Uses of cost information

In principle, cost accounting is a simple management tool. Its objective is to plan and record costs to assist in controlling and analyzing an organization. Managers can facilitate control by comparing the planned cost of some activity with its actual cost. For example, they may discover that:

A turbine blade that should require 2.0 hours of machine time actually required 2.2 hours.

Integrated circuits expected to cost $4.00 actually cost $3.50 each.

Planned expenses for a marketing department were $350,000, while actual expenses amounted to $330,000.

Each of these situations signals a problem that may require managerial attention. A good cost system raises a red flag so that management can focus its attention on potential problems. It also provides information for analysis.

Associating cost information with products or product groups makes analysis easier. This supports external analyses, such as pricing and product-mix decisions. Managers can also use such data for analyzing internal operations, such as equipment acquisition and changes in the production process or in product design. Control and analysis are the primary

uses for cost information, and the information is straightforward in most cases.

Limitations

As simple as cost accounting is conceptually, implementation can involve major problems. Product costs mirror both purchases and the production process. Thus, cost accounting can be extremely difficult in complex production settings like those of an integrated manufacturing company or a hospital, where it is difficult to associate costs with products or segments of the production process. In such cases, inaccurate product costs often lead to weak analysis, while inaccurate costs for production areas can lead to weak control. Equally serious is the familiar problem of assigning fixed overhead costs to products, which lessens the value of cost information for analysis.

Inputs

Exhibit I gives an overview of the information a cost system can provide. Inputs are the cost categories of an income statement. Assigning costs to departments, such as engineering, marketing, or finance – or determining total material and labor assigned to a department – is relatively simple. These cost summaries are usually sufficient to satisfy external reporting requirements even though an organization has poor cost control or limited product-cost information.

It is often far more difficult, however, to control material and labor costs incurred in production. Ideally in an effective cost system, managers should be able to compare actual and planned costs in detail by department, by employee, by work station, and by product. Frequently, however, only limited comparisons are possible; what can be provided at reasonable cost depends on the setting. For example, physicians, electronics repair technicians, chefs, or others in complex service organizations may perform 20 tasks each hour. Recording how they spend their time might take longer than performing the tasks themselves and could interfere with operations.

Manufacturers of complex products, such as automobiles, often encounter an equally difficult problem. Material and labor used by production departments are not recorded as expenses; they become part of the cost of a product. Associating costs with products is hard to do because most production costs are first associated with parts or subassemblies, and these components can be used in many different finished products. The complex transaction details

Exhibit I   **Input-output cost matrix for a
computer manufacturer**

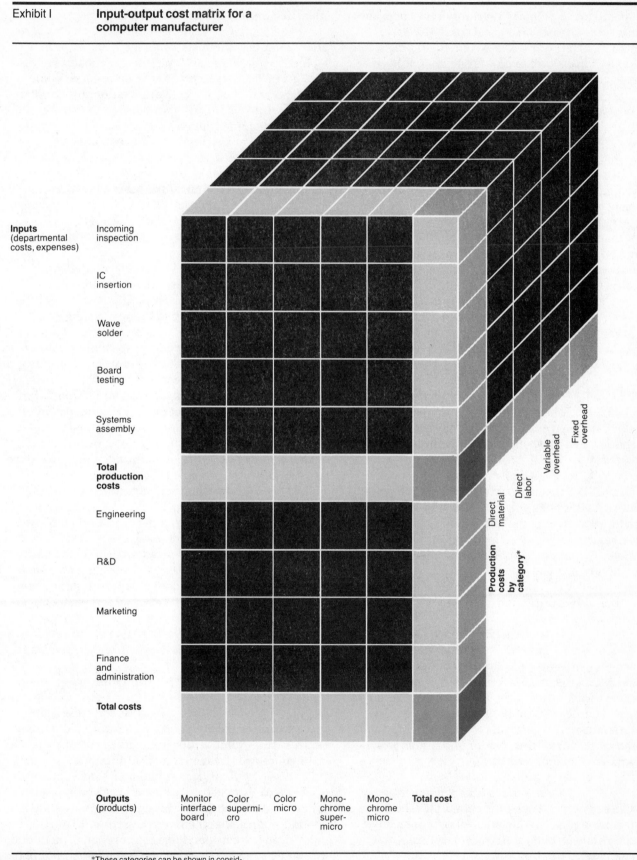

Inputs
(departmental
costs, expenses)

Incoming
inspection

IC
insertion

Wave
solder

Board
testing

Systems
assembly

**Total
production
costs**

Engineering

R&D

Marketing

Finance
and
administration

Total costs

Outputs
(products)

Monitor
interface
board

Color
supermi-
cro

Color
micro

Mono-
chrome
super-
micro

Mono-
chrome
micro

Total cost

**Production
costs
by
category***

Direct
material

Direct
labor

Variable
overhead

Fixed
overhead

*These categories can be shown in consid-
erably more detail, such as machine overhead, labor overhead, or material overhead.

needed to describe such a process can lead to major errors in product cost and in inventory cost. For example, an electronic instrument that costs $10,190 according to a company's cost system may in reality cost $11,500. In essence the cost system has leaks that are detected only by taking a physical inventory.

Outputs

The accuracy of product cost information is highly dependent on setting. *Exhibit I* shows cost inputs associated with products (or outputs) and categorized by cost type, such as material, labor, and variable or fixed overhead. Measuring variable costs by product presents a number of problems that are specific to a setting, while cost allocations present more general problems:

Variable costs. In some instances, it is easy to associate variable costs with products. Consider, for example, an injection molding company producing an order of auto taillight covers. Here direct labor cost can easily be recorded by product, since one employee will spend several days on a product or job. Material is also issued and recorded by product, so measuring material cost is similarly straightforward. And this is how some believe costs are measured in most situations.

Integrated manufacturing companies, however, usually produce parts and subassemblies for inventory. As it is not known at the time of production which finished product will use which part or subassembly, associating costs with products is hard. Variable costs also present a problem for complex service organizations. As mentioned, it is also often difficult to measure variable costs without interfering with operations. In cases like these, managers often use estimated costs.

Allocated costs. Although some academics consider fixed overhead allocations irrelevant for operating decisions, allocations are widely used in product pricing decisions, apparently as estimates of long-run variable costs. Although allocated costs are in no sense the true cost of anything, they may be the best estimates of the long-run cost of producing a product, and are useful for this reason. Allocations present well-known problems, however—

☐   If a year's production volume is unusually high or low, fixed overhead per unit will be unusually low or high. To avoid this effect, a company can base overhead costs on the normal production volume.

☐   Fixed costs are based on historical costs in most cases. It is often useful to know the value of fixed costs if a company has new equipment or equipment of the same age as that of a competitor.

☐   While there is no single, correct way to allocate costs to products, some methods are more sensible than others. For example, most companies allocate overhead costs based only on labor costs. While satisfactory in the past, with automation this method of accounting incorrectly shows lower overhead costs for products turned out on expensive equipment and therefore higher overhead for other products.

Operation constraints

Ideally, a cost system provides both actual and standard costs (see the insert for a discussion of the calculation and use of these two types of costs). Some managers have a strong preference for actual costs, but in certain circumstances it is impractical to measure actual product costs. In these cases it may be necessary to use standard costs and calculate variances in order to estimate actual costs.

Companies can determine variable production costs by several methods. They can record costs by job, batch, department, or individual operation. Alternatively, they can make cost estimates, which they can use without verification, or which they can partially verify by spot checks. It is often reasonable to use estimates for small companies or for simple production processes.

Product types and production processes mainly determine the appropriate cost system for a company, and focusing on these two factors can narrow the range of options quickly. *Exhibit II* classifies products and companies into eight groups by type and process and shows how environment affects what is feasible in a cost system.

Job-order production

A job-order production process is usually the setting where it is easy to install a cost system and where its value is seen as highest, since many such companies need frequent cost information.

Consider a cold-drawn steel company that processes steel bars to customer specifications. These bars may be drawn through a die, heat-treated, ground, polished, straightened, and cut in 10 or 15 operations. Since each operation requires enough labor that recording time by job and by work station is a minor inconvenience, a job-order cost system is appropriate. Material scrap can also be recorded by job and by work station. This kind of system provides actual cost by operation and by product. If companies establish standard costs, they can easily compare actual costs with those standards. If a job requires only minor labor or many short operations, recording actual cost by job is usually impractical, in which case an informal cost system may be preferable.

A job-order cost system provides detailed cost control and accurate product costs. Since managers have a choice of using standard or actual costs, there is little else that one could want from a cost system. And that is the problem: it works so well, and so inexpensively, that managers try to use job-order cost systems in inappropriate settings such as assembly operations.

Discrete-part products

The most technically difficult setting for cost accounting is discrete-part production by batch or by assembly process. Examples include computers, electronics equipment, or other products with numerous component parts. A relatively uniform cost system based on detailed production records has always been possible for such products. With high-speed, low-cost computers such systems are now practical.

Discrete-part products produced by batch or assembly process are not well suited to job-order costing or to determining actual costs. The manufacturer usually assembles customer orders from parts and subassemblies that have been produced before the order is received, so the cost of the order cannot be recorded by job. Actual product costs are also difficult to calculate since they require a record of actual costs for each part and subassembly.

Standard cost systems provide satisfactory results for a batch process. Companies can record variances either for each batch produced in a department or for each operation or work station. The latter method provides more detailed control but is far more expensive.

Computer cost systems that calculate variance by batch are not generally available in standard software but a company can design and install a fairly inexpensive tailor-made system in a few months. Operations cost systems, however, are far more expensive and time-consuming to develop. Standard software packages for batch or operations cost systems are included as modules in a few materials requirements planning (MRP) systems. The cost of a computerized MRP system, including hardware, is several hundred thousand dollars for a company with a few hundred employees, and implementation may require two years to refine standard costs and production records.

An alternative approach is to use standard costs in an informal cost system. As standard costs in this case are not compared with actual inputs, they may be inaccurate and lead to large inventory errors. Such a system is inexpensive and simple to maintain, however, and thus is a reasonable choice for small manufacturing companies.

Another problem in setting up an accounting system for discrete-part products is cost aggregation. Because costs are accumulated through various levels of production, many cost systems, especially older ones, aggregate them, thus making it difficult to separate product costs into material, labor, and overhead components or into variable and fixed costs. A well-designed cost system can easily overcome this problem.

Cost accounting for discrete-part products produced by an assembly process has all the problems of batch production plus another: an assembly line usually produces simultaneously several models, so it can be hard to associate material or labor with a particular batch.

One option is to calculate an overall variance for the production department for a given period, such as a month. Variances by department may provide accurate product-cost information, and such a system is inexpensive. It provides relatively weak financial control, however, since disaggregating variances within a department may be a problem.

It is also possible to calculate production variances by work station using an operations-cost system, or to use standard costs without verification. As in the case of a batch-production process, a cost system that provides detailed variances for an assembly line is expensive, while using standards without verification provides inaccurate product-cost information and almost no cost control.

Few material inputs

With few material inputs, cost accounting has few technical problems. Where the time spent on a task is brief, however, obtaining detailed operating information is usually not feasible and cost accounting information is based either on estimates or on industrial engineering kinds of studies. With medium-volume operations, installing a simple actual-cost system is often practical. But where volumes are low, usually only an informal cost system, without comparison to actual inputs, can be justified.

High-volume processes with few material inputs are often so automated and so straightforward from a cost-accounting view that managers can control costs and estimate product costs without a formal cost system. Products usually have one or two

Exhibit II   **Framework for cost systems**

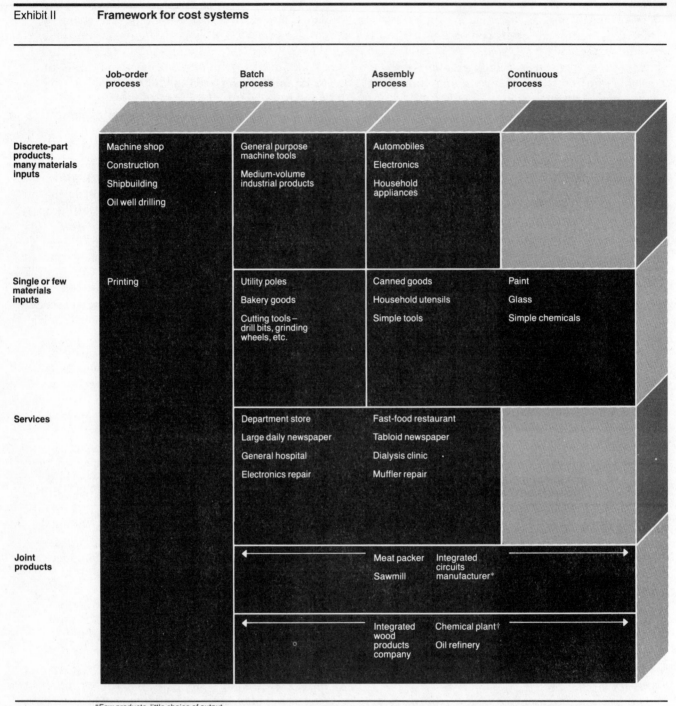

	Job-order process	Batch process	Assembly process	Continuous process
Discrete-part products, many materials inputs	Machine shop Construction Shipbuilding Oil well drilling	General purpose machine tools Medium-volume industrial products	Automobiles Electronics Household appliances	
Single or few materials inputs	Printing	Utility poles Bakery goods Cutting tools – drill bits, grinding wheels, etc.	Canned goods Household utensils Simple tools	Paint Glass Simple chemicals
Services		Department store Large daily newspaper General hospital Electronics repair	Fast-food restaurant Tabloid newspaper Dialysis clinic Muffler repair	
Joint products		Meat packer Integrated circuits Sawmill manufacturer* Integrated Chemical plant† wood products Oil refinery company		

*Few products, little choice of output.
†Many products, wide choice of output.

material inputs and the labor tends to be minor. An experienced manager can estimate product costs if he or she knows average costs of raw material and rates of production. Although managers typically use process-cost systems, these provide little information not obtainable by real time measures. In such settings, cost systems are generally used to verify other information and to value inventory. Physical measures of activity can replace financial measures, since costs are effectively controlled through use of gauges and computer displays.

Service companies

High-volume service companies can use effective cost systems, while service companies with low volumes present some of the most difficult problems in cost accounting. Consider a high-volume fast-food restaurant chain. Since the menu is limited to a few prepared items, material inputs can be recorded on a daily basis. Similarly, the labor involved tends to be simple and repetitive, so it is easily recorded in detail.

In such a setting, managers can tightly control costs and accurately measure product costs. In addition, such cost systems are inexpensive and do not interfere with service.

A general hospital lies at the other extreme; it is generally a low-volume service organization. Consider the cost of a nurse. He or she may spend an average of three minutes with each patient, performing, say, five functions for someone with a complex illness. Recording time spent for each function could require that a hospital double its nursing staff. Similar costing problems exist for physicians because of the complexities of diagnosis and treatment.

The shift from reimbursing for cost to reimbursing a fixed amount for each procedure is causing hospitals to emphasize output cost accounting. Periodically studying various parts of a hospital's operations can help administrators lower costs. For example, keeping detailed records on the obstetrics department for a one- or two-month period may indicate certain areas where time spent on care can be reduced, where an alternate treatment is preferable, or where fewer drugs or supplies can be used. Such a study can also provide standard product costs.

These industrial engineering types of studies are unlikely to lead to highly detailed, general-purpose cost measurement systems such as a discrete-part products operation might use. Instead, hospitals can use illness acuity profiles to develop a simplified standard cost system. On the basis of the illness and the acuity, patients are ranked on their expected use of perhaps ten different hospital services, such as monitoring, treatment, or feeding. These usage profiles help to plan staffing. No records need be kept of actual time spent servicing each patient or of actual time by hospital service. However, the hospital can compare the total actual staffing for each floor with the planned staffing as a rough check on efficiency.

Most specialized service companies face similar problems. Cost systems that record actual product costs are likely to prove unworkable because it is difficult to specify the product and because labor time is too brief to justify recording.

Joint products

In many situations a production process yields several products from one or a few material inputs, and it is possible to monitor costs through process controls. Analyzing product costs, however, presents difficulties.

Let's look at a manufacturer who produces a single model of an integrated circuit. Some circuits are of sufficiently high quality to meet military specifications while others are suitable only for commercial use. If the military buys a unit for $10 while a commercial unit sells for $5, should product costs be allocated so that the cost of a military circuit is twice that of a commercial circuit? Since the objective is to earn the maximum profit from a group of products, how costs are allocated to joint products is irrelevant.

If there is a choice of output, for example in a petroleum refinery, determining product costs is even more complicated. When the company's objective is to use a raw material in such a way that it will generate the most profit, cost accounting has little value. Instead, managers can use mathematical programming techniques to determine both the level of production and what should be produced.

Selecting a system

Most organizations consider a range of options when selecting a cost system. Cost controls can be extensive or limited; standard or actual product costs can be accurate measures or only reasonable estimates. As we have seen, several factors influence these choices, and there are often conflicts between what is best for control and for analysis. In most cases it is control, based on a company's organizational design, that dictates the choice.

Cost control

In some cases, detailed control systems are too expensive, interfere with operations, and reduce initiative or creativity. Weak systems, however, lead to waste, inefficiency, and irrational pricing. What is appropriate depends on a number of factors:

Market environment. Cost control is likely to be of strategic importance for undifferenti-

Actual and standard product costs

Actual cost

Wages paid for direct labor and the invoice price of materials make up actual product cost. Its calculation is not difficult in a job-order production process or in certain high-volume processes. In most other cases, determining actual product cost is too expensive to be justified.

Standard cost

The main reason for using standard cost is that calculating actual product cost can be prohibitively expensive. Three issues are important to understanding standard costs:

1

How they are established. Standards can be based on industrial engineering-type studies, or on simple estimates by those familiar with an operation.

2

The level at which they are set. Standards can be set at an ideal, rarely attainable, level or they can be an approximation of actual costs, in which case they are sometimes called predetermined estimates. Choice of level is a management option involving factors such as motivation, control, analysis, and taxation.

3

How they are used. In a formal standard cost system, managers can use standards to evaluate actual costs. Even when determining actual product costs is impractical, standard costs can be usefully compared with actual department or work center costs.

In both cases, variances from actual cost can be used to improve standards or be associated with standard product costs to approximate actual product costs. The variance between actual and standard cost may be calculated by job, batch, department, or individual production operation. The more detailed the variance, the more expensive it will be to design and install a cost system.

Alternatively, standard costs may be used without a formal cost system. In this case, managers do not calculate variances, so that verifying the accuracy of standards is difficult. Although systems using only standard costs provide very little cost control, they are often reasonable choices for small manufacturers or service companies whose production processes are too varied, or of too short a duration, to measure.

ated, low-margin products. For example, parts suppliers to the auto industry must meet delivery and quality targets, but, other than those constraints, cost control is probably the single most important factor in a profitable operation. In contrast, cost control may be important for unique, high-margin products but is rarely crucial to a company's success. Examples include expensive liquor and cosmetics businesses, where marketing dominates cost control.

Competitive strategy. Companies whose objective is market leadership in volume need cost control more than those with strategies of providing innovative specialty products. Consider, for example, two medium-sized electronics companies, both well run and highly profitable. One has a dominant market position and a stable product line. The company calculates variances between actual and standard costs in detail, and its cost system is extremely accurate. The other company sells innovative products using state-of-the-art technology, so product life is short. Its management also emphasizes cost control, but it calculates variances in less detail, and its cost system is less accurate.

Product cycle. At the beginning of a product cycle, products tend to offer unique features and to sell for high margins. Later, as a product matures and the process is standardized, margins are reduced, so cost control becomes more important. As complex cost systems may require several years to install and test, managers must anticipate the need for cost control.

Size. Formal systems, with their requisite record keeping and the discipline of maintaining production records, can be burdensome for a small company. Fortunately, knowledgeable managers can often control and analyze costs without detailed systems. As a company grows, it is more likely to have the staff necessary to maintain a formal cost system. It is also more likely to need one, since even the best managers are unable to control costs intuitively. This is especially true for complex service and discrete-part manufacturing organizations.

Cost structure. The proportion each cost bears to total production cost is an important factor in deciding which costs to control. For a product whose labor cost is 5% of production cost and material cost is 80%, control of material costs is obviously important. And yet many companies have elaborate systems to control minor elements of total cost while ignoring more important cost elements. As companies change from labor-intensive to highly automated operations, many still continue to concentrate on controlling labor costs.

Cost analysis

Standard and actual product costs can vary from highly accurate numbers to rough estimates. What is reasonable depends on a number of factors:

Sales volume. If sales are high, and if a company has few products, prices will probably be set to maximize the marginal contribution, as microeconomic texts recommend. An example is a soft drink in a fast-food restaurant chain. A company may determine that a small soft drink should sell for 45 cents in order to maximize profit. In this case variable product cost must be accurate, while cost allocations are of little value.

Where sales volume is low, and where a company has many products, the effort required to set price in detail using economic theory is rarely justified. Instead, managers often set price using both variable and allocated costs as an estimate of long-run cost. For example, a company that repairs electronic equipment and handles over 70 products from various manufacturers sets prices to cover all costs associated with a product and to provide a profit margin that varies depending on economic conditions.

Differences in how products use resources. Cost allocations are estimates of a product's use of resources. Those estimates can be very inaccurate for external financial reporting, so allocating overhead on direct labor may be adequate. If a company uses product costs for pricing, however, it is important that it allocate costs in reasonable relation to a product's use of resources. Thus, overhead may be allocated on material cost and machine time, as well as on labor cost.

Improved cost allocations are especially important for complex products, since it is often difficult to intuitively adjust allocated costs. That is, for a simple machined product a manager may know that one product required one hour on an inexpensive machine, while another required 15 minutes on a highly automated machine. If the cost system allocates four times as much overhead to the first product, a manager can easily make an informal adjustment to each product's overhead cost. For complex products, produced in many operations at many locations, such adjustments are often infeasible. Instead, a more detailed cost system is needed.

Market position. A market leader of a company with an exclusive product can usually establish price. If product costs are inaccurate, even a company with a well-considered pricing strategy will incorrectly price its products. For example, when several manufacturing companies installed improved cost systems, they found that standard and estimated actual costs were so inaccurate that some products sold at less than variable costs. Others were priced so high as to openly invite competition.

A company in a weak market position can sometimes use such cost information to competitive advantage. In many instances it can find mispriced market segments and then shift to the more profitable product lines.

Extent of fixed cost. If fixed costs are a high percentage of total costs, product costs are usually unimportant for pricing, as in the case of oil shippers, oil drilling companies, airlines, and software companies. Because variable costs are so low in these businesses, volume has a dominant effect on profitability. The fact that industry capacity is relatively fixed in the intermediate term causes changes in demand to lead to major swings in prices. It is these major economic factors, rather than allocated costs, that influence price. As manufacturing companies shift to highly automated plants, they can expect to face the same problem that airlines have experienced for years.

Many managers consider cost accounting to be a straightforward, general-purpose management tool. In practice, however, it is complex and related to the setting. Changes in computer technology now offer a great opportunity to improve cost systems in certain settings, such as batch or assembly production of discrete-part products. Elsewhere there is less scope for major advances and the challenge is to develop a cost system that is reasonable for the circumstances. By recognizing the relationship between a cost system and its setting, it is possible to improve a company's cost system significantly and, in turn, the working relationship between the accounting group and other departments. ▽

Reprint 85113

*A fast way to decide if your cost system
gives you bad information*

You Need a
New Cost System When...

by Robin Cooper

By now it's well publicized—if not obvious—that many companies' cost accounting systems are falling down on the job. They give managers incorrect product costing information, or they inundate managers with irrelevant cost information, or they fail to measure the things that really count. Strategies may be conceptually brilliant, but if they are based on faulty information about the cost of a product, they are likely to fail in the marketplace. Many have.

But redesigning a cost system is expensive and time consuming. Do you really have to do it? There are two ways of finding out.

An obsolete cost system sends many signals, so one way to discover if you need a new system is to learn how to read those signals. (See the insert for a definition of an obsolete cost system.)

Cost systems don't become obsolete overnight. They gradually outlive their usefulness as they fail to adapt to change. So a second way to tell if your system has deteriorated is to analyze the changes that have occurred in your organization and in its environment since you first implemented the system.

It's Time to Redesign Your System If You Notice That...

...functional managers want to drop seemingly profitable lines. Production managers know when a product is troublesome. And marketing managers know when a product isn't priced competitively. You can use their knowledge to test your cost system. Ask them to list the ten established products they would most like to drop. If there is nothing special about those items, and yet they still show high profits, the cost system may be failing to capture their true complexity.

...profit margins are hard to explain. Managers should be able to give simple explanations of profit margins: "We have the best production technologies"; "We have lower production volumes"; "Nobody else makes that product"; or "We set the standard and make a premium for doing so." In one company, the production manager was under constant pressure to make a certain new product more cheaply. He couldn't explain the high costs. He was confident that he was doing a good job and believed the product should be competitive. Years later a revised cost system showed that because the product used more direct labor than any other, it was being charged too much overhead. It was in fact the company's most profitable line. Unfortunately, by then, competitors had introduced similar products and the opportunity was lost.

...hard-to-make products show big profits. A good test of a cost system is an item that's harder to make or requires more inspection or rework than others.

Robin Cooper is associate professor of business administration at the Harvard Business School and a fellow of the Institute of Chartered Accountants in England and Wales.

What Is an Obsolete Cost System?

A cost system shouldn't necessarily measure absolutely everything down to the finest degree. Taking infinitesimal measurements of each bit of material and each second of direct labor can be expensive and time consuming. The expense is necessary only when the consequences of relying on inaccurate information are severe. When, for instance, margins are paper thin and the market moves quickly, basing decisions on inaccurate cost data can put a company out of business in a hurry. In other situations, highly accurate numbers are less important, and the company shouldn't spend a lot of money to get them.

A good cost system trades off the cost of measurement and the cost of errors from inaccurate information in a way that minimizes total cost (see accompanying graphs). As an economist would put it, the optimal system exists at the point where the marginal cost of improving the system's accuracy exactly equals the marginal benefit.

An optimal cost system is a moving target. Competitive conditions are dynamic, so the cost of errors changes. Similarly, as information-processing technology changes, so does the cost of measurement.

It is important to remember that product diversity has a great deal to do with accuracy. As diversity increases—as high volume is mixed with low volume, or labor intensity is mixed with automation—costs are more likely to be skewed. To achieve the same level of accuracy, companies will have to spend more on measurements than when products were more homogeneous. If they don't, their cost systems will be obsolete.

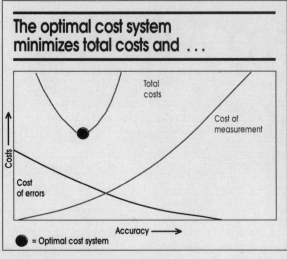

The optimal cost system minimizes total costs and . . .

Total costs
Cost of measurement
Cost of errors
Accuracy →
Costs
● = Optimal cost system

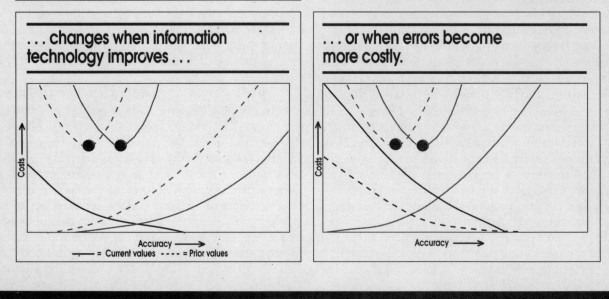

. . . changes when information technology improves . . .

Costs
Accuracy →
——— = Current values   - - - - = Prior values

. . . or when errors become more costly.

Costs
Accuracy →

Such products will have higher than average costs and, unless they are priced at a premium, will have low margins. If they are not premium priced but appear to be highly profitable, the cost system is failing to report their true cost.

...departments have their own cost systems. When functional managers have completely lost faith in the official cost system, they may develop systems of their own. Personal computers make it fairly easy to do. The design engineers in an electronics company didn't trust the numbers the cost system produced. Bad or complex designs came out looking like big profit makers, while products the engineers knew to be well designed appeared to be losers. The engineering department responded by developing its own system for costing products.

Where the official system used direct labor to allocate costs, the private system used a number of different bases. Also, the engineers tracked costs they considered to be product related but that the official system treated as period expenses. The department ignored the official system and used its private system to steer design work.

...the accounting department spends a lot of time on special projects. Some decisions require more accurate information than others. A decision on outsourcing a high-volume product, for example, is important enough to warrant more detailed and accurate cost data. Accounting departments often set up special teams to study such situations. But the cost system—if it's doing its job—should provide

Managers can quickly diagnose an obsolete cost system by checking the symptoms.

managers with much of the information they need. If its failure to do so makes lengthy special studies routine, the cost system is probably obsolete. This was the case at one company, where half of the accounting staff was working on special projects, some of which took more than six months to complete.

...you have a high-margin niche all to yourself. Unless barriers to entry exist, companies should expect competition. If there is none, the cost system may be reporting fictitious margins. One company found that as its niche expanded, overall margins fell. A redesigned cost system showed that products the company thought were earning high profits were actually losing money. Another company discovered that a competitor was buying its products and then repackaging and selling them. The company's selling price, based on faulty cost information, was lower than the competitor's production cost.

...competitors' prices are unrealistically low. When other successful companies, especially smaller ones, charge less for items you produce in high volume, your cost system is suspect. It is likely the system averages product costs among your high- and low-volume items. The smaller company probably makes products whose production volumes are similar, so averaging creates less cost distortion.

...customers don't mind price increases. Customers will certainly never ask for price increases. But if they aren't surprised when increases come, they may know more about your costs than you. Even if they

complain, they may think, "It's about time" and pay the higher prices willingly. After all, they may have explored making the product themselves or have information on competitors' costs. When one company sensed that its prices were too low, it raised them by 25%. The market didn't flinch. Customers paid the higher prices without complaint; sales volume dropped off only slightly. The market confirmed management's intuition that the cost information was wrong.

...the results of bids are hard to explain. Unless the market is chaotic, managers should be able to estimate the competitiveness of their bids. In particular, they should be able to set high bids for business they don't really want and low bids for business that's important to them. But a company's bids are often based on the cost information it gets internally. If that information is faulty, the company will have no idea how its bid compares with competitors'. When one cutting-tool manufacturer kept winning high bids and losing low bids, the president suspected that the cost system was the culprit. A new cost system solved the problem.

...vendor bids are lower than expected. Companies that are considering outsourcing can compare vendors' bids with their own costs to tell if their cost system is working well. If the bid price varies widely from the cost of making the product, the cost system may be at fault. In one case, the vendor bid was below the variable cost of the product, yet there were no indications that the vendor was that much more efficient. A special team looked into the matter and found that the product could in fact be made more cheaply in-house—despite the cost system's message to the contrary.

...reported costs change because of new financial accounting regulations. Systems designed with one goal in mind generally don't do a good job of meeting others.[1] A system that aims to meet financial reporting requirements probably distorts costs. If a new GAAP regulation changes your costs even when materials prices and manufacturing costs are constant, chances are you tailored your system to meet financial reporting requirements—not to provide accurate cost information.

Your System May Be Obsolete If You've Experienced...

...increased automation. When direct labor is used as an allocation base, the introduction of automated production processes such as flexible machining systems can cause the system to fail. The new machin-

1. See Robert S. Kaplan, "One Cost System Isn't Enough," HBR January-February 1988, p.61.

ery uses less direct labor but usually requires more support for programming and engineering. Products made through automation tend not to be charged enough overhead, while products manufactured conventionally are charged too much.

One company had completely revamped its production process to move from machines that required continuous direct-labor supervision to machines that required virtually no operator attendance. The direct-labor-based system failed to capture the economics of the new production process because it didn't allocate overhead to products made on the new machines. A system based on machine hours corrected the problem. Reported costs of some products changed by as much as 30%.

It's time for a new cost system when engineering develops one of its own.

An integrated-circuit manufacturer introduced a new line of chips, which was a good strategic fit but did not fit well with the cost system. Production of the new product was highly automated, so when it came time to allocate overhead, as always, on the basis of direct labor hours, the new product got off easy. The system didn't reflect the new line's more intensive use of the costly automated machines. The cost system was distorted. Even worse, the existing products were charged with too much overhead and appeared unprofitable. Subsequently, the company moved their production offshore.

...changes in the use of support functions. If a new product requires different kinds of support from existing lines—more detailed inspection, for example, or longer setups—the amount of overhead allocated to it will likely be incorrect. These distortions can creep in slowly. For example, one company introduced a new line of plastic products to complement its sheet metal business. Initially, volume was relatively low, so little distortion arose from allocating the overhead needed only for metal fabrication to both plastic and metal products. Over time, however, sales of the plastic products increased dramatically, and the distortion became serious.

...changes in product market strategy. The decision to market in a low-volume niche means smaller production volume. In contrast, the decision to move from experimental parts to production parts means higher volume. Most cost systems are designed with one type of production in mind and don't differentiate well between the overhead consumed by high- and low-volume products. When production vol-

umes vary widely in the same company, cost distortion arises. If production volumes are fairly similar—say, volume of one product is no more than five times that of any other—product costs will probably be accurate. Accuracy falls off rapidly as the range grows to more than 10 to 1.[2]

One company produced some products in batches of under 50 and others in batches of more than 1,000. Its traditional direct-labor-based cost system grossly undercosted the low-volume products and made them appear more profitable than they were. The company thought its product strategy—trying to be everything to everybody—was working, but the economics were misleading. Year after year, profits fell, and the company was eventually taken over.

In contrast, another company was forced to adopt the strategy of producing low-volume, customized products because competitors had an overwhelming labor cost advantage. To ensure that the orders it accepted for low-volume items were truly profitable, the company introduced a new cost system that more appropriately traced overhead to high- and low-volume products. The new cost system helped the company implement its new strategy successfully.

...simplification of manufacturing processes. Changes in the production environment don't necessarily require more complex cost systems. The introduction of new and simpler production philosophies, such as just-in-time (JIT) or cellular manufacturing, can make a needlessly complex system obsolete. In one company, the cost system measured the value of work in process at every inventory stage, requiring hundreds of thousands of measurements a year. But the introduction of JIT reduced inventory levels so much that those measurements were no longer important.

Cellular manufacturing has the same effect on old cost systems. This manufacturing approach creates a series of mini-factories, each specializing in similar items. Companies should be able to trace overhead directly to the mini-factories and then spread those costs evenly over all the units they produce. A cost system that traces costs to individual products is probably obsolete.

...intensified competition. When competition heats up, so does the chance that a competitor will take advantage of a poor pricing decision. The increased risk associated with poor cost information can make a system obsolete. When a product is overcosted, its profit margin will look deceptively unattractive. If a competitor gives chase to the product, the company may mistakenly decide not to defend its position. Alternatively, prices set too high because

2. See Robin Cooper and Robert S. Kaplan, "Measure Costs Right: Make the Right Decisions," HBR September-October 1988, p. 96.

they're overcosted might attract competitors that would otherwise have faced a higher barrier to entry. One company redesigned its cost system and discovered that a particular product line was considerably more profitable than it had thought. To avoid attracting competition, the company increased the discount, added more field support, and increased advertising spending.

When companies earn a reasonable overall margin, they often don't worry about the margins individual products make. In the face of stiffer competition, though, management needs reliable cost information to act confidently. Executives must know how much leeway they have in underpricing the competition and at what point a product line is not worth saving.

One manufacturing company introduced a new system just in the nick of time. Its old system had been generating huge year-end variances, so the president astutely targeted the cost system for redesign. Soon after, the industry went into a slump and prices fell dramatically. The company, with its new knowledge of product costs, was able to cut prices more aggressively than other players. It picked up the business of several failed competitors and in certain product lines increased its market share permanently by as much as 300%.

...unbundling of products. For many years one company had bundled two products together: apparel fastener machines, which the customer rented, and apparel fasteners, which the customer attached to their products using the machines. The rental fee for the machines was purposely set low to attract customers, who became captive buyers of the fasteners. The price of the fasteners was set high enough to cover their costs as well as the unrecovered costs of the machines. The cost system traced all overhead costs to fasteners and none to the machines.

On the surface, the system worked fine. Customers were happy and loyal. But when the company redesigned the cost system so it separated costs of the two types of products, it became clear that the cost system was actually sending highly distorted signals. Because some of the fasteners were labor intensive, the old system had attributed a disproportionate amount of overhead (including the cost of the attaching machines) to them. Over the years, the company had put little effort into these product lines and consequently walked away from attractive markets.

...deregulation. Under regulation, a company doesn't set the prices; the regulators do. Companies make profits by controlling overall efficiency. Deregulation increases a company's competitive choices but can make a cost system useless. When companies have new freedom to "cherry pick" products, accurate knowledge of costs is invaluable. One railroad company, for example, when faced with deregulation, introduced a new cost system that for the first time in the company's history reported the cost of a freight-car move from city to city. Its existing cost system reported the cost of each function (switching, locomotive repair, and the like) but not the cost of a move. Knowledge of these costs allowed the railroad to compete more effectively with other railroads and trucking companies.

Some situations mimic the effects of deregulation, like when a captive supplier is allowed or forced to compete on the outside. An internal transfer pricing system, for instance, acts

FIRST AMERICAN BANK OF THE SOVIET UNION

ТАКСИ

much like a regulated pricing system. One company that recently began to compete in the open market discovered that because of a faulty cost system, its pricing attracted the business it was least interested in and turned away the business it really wanted. The company secured sales of low-volume, complex products instead of the high-volume, simple products for which its production facility was designed. A new cost system corrected the problem and allowed the company to bid more aggressively on high-volume business.

...technological improvements. Systems can become obsolete if they fail to take advantage of technical improvements that permit more efficient data gathering and analysis. The introduction of a computerized, production floor scheduling system, for example, captures considerably more information about the products. This information can go into the cost system at virtually no cost.

Similarly, numerically controlled equipment, especially when controlled by a central computer, increases the availability of machine-readable information. Setup time and run times can be measured directly at no extra cost. Remote sensing technology, such as bar coding, can also provide lots of new information at little additional cost.

...changes in strategy and behavioral goals. Sometimes management changes its strategy and therefore wants to encourage and reward different behavior. The cost system doesn't always adapt. One

> ## The system is outdated when every decision requires a special accounting team.

company was successful because of its technological innovation. When the market sent signals that cost – not just technical superiority – was important, the company decided to pay more attention to efficient designs. It urged its engineers to stop designing from the ground up and to incorporate some of the parts already in use. The old cost system couldn't track such things as how many part numbers were used, so there was no way to identify expensive products made with low-volume or unique components. The company designed its new system with this important new variable in mind.

Another company's strategy moved toward products with very short life cycles. Designing products that could be manufactured economically in small batches became critical. In particular, the company

needed to compare the cost of inserting different types of components both manually and automatically. A new cost system enabled it to do that.

Another company bought an expensive piece of test equipment to improve product quality. But the old cost system treated the machine as overhead. The work force took advantage of this "free" work center by building complex products on it. A new cost system ensured that workers put the new equipment to best use by making the test area a cost center and charging products an hourly rate for using it.

Is It Time?

The mere presence of symptoms doesn't mean the cost system is obsolete. A product may have inexplicably low profit margins because the cost system is obsolete – or because a competitor has adopted a penetration strategy. It helps to think about the internal and external changes that make a cost system obsolete. They provide more clues to whether your system needs fixing. Checking for symptoms and looking for changes that may have caused them gives a good indication of the effectiveness of your current system. If you find no symptoms, the system is doing fine. If you observe several symptoms and know what probably caused them, it's time for a redesign.

The hard part is when you detect only one or two symptoms. Then the call is more difficult to make. One way to proceed is to set up a pilot cost system for a single product line and compare the numbers with those the existing system produces. If the results differ widely, a redesign is in order.

Remember that because conditions keep changing, managers should evaluate their systems every few years. They don't necessarily have to design a new system that often. Before a company plunges into redesign it should be sure to analyze the investment. The potential savings – the difference between the total costs of the existing system and the total costs of a new one – should exceed the cost of developing and implementing the new one.

A cost system, with modifications along the way, should last about a decade. But at some point, you can no longer patch up and add on to the system. Companies may not want to face up to the fact that their cost systems need to be redesigned, but if they don't, they may face far more severe consequences. A business that doesn't know what its products really cost won't be in business for long.

Are managers getting the information they need to value inventory, control operations, and measure product costs?

One Cost System Isn't Enough

by ROBERT S. KAPLAN

Many companies now recognize that their cost systems are inadequate for today's powerful competition. Systems designed mainly to value inventory for financial and tax statements are not giving managers the accurate and timely information they need to promote operating efficiencies and measure product costs.

In response, they have tried to redesign their present systems, but results have been disappointing:

☐ One chemical company's system did a good job of estimating full product costs but could not be used for cost control. It gathered product costs at each production stage and cumulatively absorbed all variances along the production trail. While the system reported actual costs for all products, it provided no information to motivate or evaluate the cost-reduction efforts of production managers.

As competition shifted to low-cost production of commodity products, the company had to develop a new cost system to give unit managers more reliable information about their production efficiency. Headquarters scrapped the old system and installed one that isolated all variances at the cost centers where

they occurred. Local managers could now observe the impact of their efficiency activities. Marketers and business managers disliked the new system, though, because they could now see only standard product costs. They had lost the actual cost information the old system supplied. After several years of bickering, the company overhauled the new system to recapture the old system's output.

☐ The components division of a heavy machinery business had an excellent system that promoted cost control and production efficiency. It yielded frequent reports on direct labor use and efficiency, scrap buildup, and department expenditures. The only information on product costs, however, came from the standard cost system used to allocate overhead for financial reporting purposes. This system had recently been redesigned so that overhead costs were allocated to products using machine hours and material dollars as well as the traditional direct-labor hour base. But even with this redesigned system, the division's attempts to seek outside customers were undermined by highly distorted product cost estimates.

Why are so many companies having such difficulty? Cost system designers have failed to recognize that their systems need to address three different functions:

Inventory valuation for financial and tax statements, allocating periodic production costs between goods sold and goods in stock.

Operational control, providing feedback to production and department managers on the resources consumed (labor, materials, energy, overhead) during an operating period.

Individual product cost measurement.

Even if cost system designers recognize how important and how different the demands of these three functions are, their efforts are blocked by senior executives' insistence on a single "official" system. And when compromises have to be made, the demands of the financial reporting function (inventory valuation) invariably triumph. The more managerially

Robert S. Kaplan is Arthur Lowes Dickinson Professor of Accounting at the Harvard Business School and professor of industrial administration at Carnegie-Mellon University. He won the 1987 award given jointly by the American Accounting Association and the American Institute of Certified Public Accountants for the most notable contribution to accounting literature, "Measuring Manufacturing Performance: A New Challenge for Management Accounting Research," Accounting Review *(October 1983). His latest book is* Relevance Lost: The Rise and Fall of Management Accounting, *with H. Thomas Johnson (Harvard Business School Press, 1987).*

relevant functions of operational control and product costing usually suffer.

Many businesses know the consequences of this dilemma all too well. Operating costs are reported too late and are too aggregated to benefit production supervisors. Managers must use product cost estimates that focus on the least important cost component—direct labor—and ignore expenses involved in designing, marketing, distributing, and servicing goods.

Businesses can no longer afford cost systems that work well only to value inventory for financial reporting. No single system can adequately cover all three functions. The demands of each differ in terms of reporting frequency, degree of allocation, nature of cost variability, system scope, and degree of objectivity (see the *Exhibit*).

The chemical company in the first example was better off than most: at least it had one system separate from its method for valuing inventory. Initially, the system estimated product costs; subsequently, the company changed it to improve operational control. Similarly, the heavy machinery company had a good, separate system for operational control, even though it could not estimate product costs well. I have observed many companies whose cost systems weren't good for either function. Executives need a better understanding of the different demands of the three cost system functions.

Inventory Valuation

Under generally accepted accounting principles, manufacturers must allocate periodic production costs to all items produced. Inventory valuation systems divide these costs—labor, materials purchases, and factory overhead—between items sold and those still in stock. Financial accounting principles do not require that assigned overhead costs be causally related to the demands of individual products, so many companies continue to use direct labor to allocate overhead, even though direct labor may account for less than 5% of total manufacturing costs. Moreover, businesses can use a single plantwide burden rate for allocating overhead to products, regardless of the diversity of their production processes.

Therefore, a company's overhead allocation scheme may not correspond to the underlying production process or to the demands individual products make on the enterprise's resources. Auditors won't question cost-of-sales or inventory valuation estimates merely because the company has used an aggregated, simplistic method for assigning overhead

costs to products. As long as the split of costs between goods sold and goods still in stock is fairly accurate, in aggregate, the needs of financial reports will have been met.

The cost system for external reporting does not, however, give managers relevant performance measurement and product cost information.

Operational Control

An operational control system must provide accurate, timely feedback to managers on their performance. The system must correspond to the unit manager's level of responsibility, control for known variations in cost behavior, and minimize the incidence of cost allocations. Cost-accounting calculations (like the allocation of overhead to products and departments, or the computation of volume variances) should not be part of a company's operational control system because they obscure the information that cost center managers need to operate effectively.

Frequency. Companies measure performance by comparing actual results against standard or budgeted levels. Comparisons can be made periodically or each time a unit of work is finished. To be most useful, however, the frequency of reported information should follow the cycle of the production process being measured. In departments producing hundreds of parts per hour, the per-unit materials, labor, machine time, and utility consumption should be reported daily or even hourly. The system for control in a support department or research lab could report on a much longer cycle.

Obviously, it is not much help to get monthly cost reports for an operation that turns out many parts per second. A manager controlling work hourly and daily does not want to receive an aggregate variance report in the middle of the subsequent month. Equally as obvious, daily or weekly cost reports would confuse departments taking several months to assemble a complex machine or performing basic research.

For operations under computer control, the digital data can be captured to record what, when, and how much was produced. Companies no longer need to collect production data with stopwatches, time clocks, and clipboards. Automatic bar-code reading of parts combined with local area networks permit continual tracking of parts and operations. Cost control systems can record these data and provide frequent, accurate reports on actual output and resource consumption.

Cost Fluctuations. Effective operational control requires an understanding of which costs are fixed and which change with short-term variations in activity. Separating costs in this way permits preparation of flexible budgets that adjust for changes in activity levels on the consumption of labor, materials, machine time, energy, and support services.

It is easier to establish a flexible budget for operational control when analysts grasp the underlying scientific or engineering laws governing the production process. They can then build the cost control system on the production standards established by the conversion process. A production process that is stable and repetitive also helps to predict the relationship between inputs and outputs. In both cases, the company can base its cost control system on a flexible budget that adjusts for costs that vary with fluctuations in short-run production activity.

Cost Allocations. Many companies routinely allocate costs to a cost center, even when the center has little or no control over them. This practice evolved because, to value inventory, all factory costs must be allocated to products. With traditional inventory costing systems, plant and overhead costs are first allocated to cost centers and then, using a cost center burden rate, allocated to products.

Once a company separates its system for measuring operating performance from that used to value inventory, however, it does not have to allocate common or noncontrollable costs to individual cost centers. Only those costs that are directly related to actions taken within a cost center and whose consumption can be accurately measured at the cost center level should be reported periodically to the unit manager.

For example, a cost center's metered demand for kilowatt-hours of electricity or pounds of steam should be assigned to that center. But if metering is difficult, a company does not improve cost control activities by allocating a factorywide utility expense to cost centers.

By avoiding allocations, the operating report can be based on accurate, objective data on the cost center's consumption of resources during a period. Ballpark estimates of the quantity of labor, machine time, and support resources used don't help managers' efficiency and productivity improvement efforts. Moreover, operating reports filled with estimated and allocated costs distract cost center managers from their primary responsibilties to monitor and control production efficiencies and to improve productivity. If headquarters occasionally needs unit managers to help monitor costs incurred by the whole division or the company, it can allocate common costs to the cost center—on a one-time basis, for information purposes only.

Nonfinancial Measurements. Cost information may, in fact, play only a minor role in operational control. A company maintains control best at the shop-floor level by frequent reports of measures like yield, defects, output, setup and throughput times, and physical inventory levels. At the department level, monthly summaries of quality control (part-per-million defect rates, percentage of items produced with no rework required), average throughput times, percentage of delivery commitments met, inventory levels, new product introduction times, and marketing and distribution statistics make up the most relevant set of performance measures. Financial measurements are useful for periodically com-

EXHIBIT
Different Functions, Different Demands

Functions	Frequency	Degree of Allocation	Scope of System	Nature of Variability	Degree of Objectivity
Inventory valuation	Monthly or quarterly	Aggregate	Factory costs	Irrelevant	High
Operational control	Daily, by unit of work accomplished	None	Responsibility center	Short-term variable and fixed	High
Product cost measurement	Annually and at major change points	Extensive, down to individual products or product lines	Entire organization, including production, marketing and distribution, engineering, service, and administration	All variable	Low

paring actual with budgeted expenditures in each department. Measures of process costs will be helpful when many inputs are combined into intermediate and finished products. But many companies rely too much on summary financial measures and ignore the powerful opportunities for continual improvement that a well-constructed set of nonfinancial operating measures can give them.

Product Cost Measurement

Even the best designed and implemented operational control system, however, can be useless for measuring product costs. Take the experience of one company in the transportation industry. By the late 1960s, the company had developed an extensive network for accumulating and reporting costs at each of its more than 5,000 cost centers. It summarized them by different classifications, geographical regions, and degree of authority for all levels of management. By comparing operating costs against budget and to the same periods in the previous year, the system provided an excellent tool for cost control and productivity improvement.

Then deregulation—and price competition—hit the company. Executives realized that none of the information in their elaborate reporting system could help them to estimate product costs. Without knowledge of product costs, the new freedom to quote prices and to enter or leave markets could have been disastrous. Fortunately, the company developed completely new systems to estimate product costs and to evaluate product and product-line profitability. The company is now prospering in its deregulated environment.

Traditional standard cost systems in manufacturing companies are designed not to measure product costs accurately but to value inventory. The standard costs usually bear no relation to the resources consumed to design, produce, market, and deliver the product. I have seen cases where a more accurate system revealed that products yielding healthy profits according to the standard cost system—with indicated margins of more than 45%—were actually losing money. Similarly, careful analyses of marketing and distribution expenses have shown that product lines, previously considered to be only breaking even, were actually among the company's most profitable.

Seriously distorted product costs can lead managers to choose a losing competitive strategy by deemphasizing and overpricing products that are highly profitable and by expanding commitments to complex, unprofitable lines. The company persists in the losing strategy because executives have no alternative sources of information to signal when product costs are distorted. Only after many years of declining market share and reduced profitability will managers learn how erroneous product costs led to poor product mix and pricing decisions.

Analysts, attempting to understand the demands a product makes on the company's resources, can start by interviewing the supervisors of production, support, logistics, and marketing departments. They must learn what creates work for the resources in these areas, the cost of performing the work, and the quantity of work demanded by individual products.

Allocations and Estimates. Extensive allocations of support department costs may be necessary to estimate the unit costs of the activities that these departments perform. In the transportation company, for example, virtually all the product costs came from an allocation process.

Product cost estimates will not have the five- and six-digit precision reported by a standard cost system. They will also be more subjective and less precise than the measurements in an operational control system. Executives of multiproduct companies will be fortunate if the first digit in their product cost estimates is valid, and they can make a reasonably good guess at the second. But the estimates will realistically approximate the *long-run* demands each product makes on the organization's resources.

Cost Variability. A company should base most of its important product decisions on estimates of the long-run, variable costs of individual products.[1] Whether costs are fixed or variable, of course, depends on the viewer's time horizon. In the short run, virtually all costs are fixed: materials have already been acquired, utilities have been turned on, and the workers have showed up for the day. Over a long period, however, costs become variable: machines and plants can be retired or sold, supervisors transferred.

Product decisions have long-term consequences for the organization. Executives should therefore consider virtually all costs to be variable when measuring product costs. That will require a new orientation for many managers. They must recognize that many costs traditionally thought of as fixed actually vary according to the diversity and complexity of products. Much manufacturing overhead, for example, comes from transactions associated with the

1. See Robin Cooper and Robert S. Kaplan, "How Cost Accounting Systematically Distorts Product Costs," in *Accounting & Management: Field Study Perspectives,* ed. William J. Bruns, Jr. and Robert S. Kaplan (Cambridge: Harvard Business School Press, 1987), p. 204.

2. See Jeffrey Miller and Thomas Vollman, "The Hidden Factory," HBR September-October 1985, p. 142.

start or finish of production, such as placing and paying for orders, receiving and inspecting purchased materials, setting up machines, moving inventory, and shipping finished goods.[2]

To reflect these costs, the system must include not only traditional volume-related measures for tracing costs to products such as labor and machine hours or materials quantities, but also measures that count setups, inspections, receipts, parts, vendors, and engineering change orders. The scheme must determine how indirect production costs vary in the long run, both with regard to production volume and to the activities necessary to produce multiple items in the same facility.

System Scope. While the typical operational control system segregates costs incurred at each responsibility center, a good product cost system should report expenses incurred across the organization's entire value chain. A product's cost includes not only the cost of factory resources to convert raw materials and purchased components to a finished item but also the cost of resources to establish the distribution channel, make the sale (including advertising and promotion), service the product, and supply support services like engineering design, process improvement, purchasing, information systems, financial and cost analysis, and general administration.

All company resources support production and sales. Even corporate expenses should be allocated to product costs, especially if they vary across lines. Legal expenses are a good example. They can vary by risks of product liability and environmental damage, or by antitrust concerns across different categories of products.

The product cost system can ignore only two classes of costs—expenses incurred that benefit future products, like basic research or development, and the expenses of idle or unused capacity. Existing financial accounting rules require that basic R&D be expensed each period. But for managerial purposes, R&D should be considered investments in future products, not costs of present products. Unused capacity is an expense for a particular period due to cyclical declines in sales, or an investment for

"In answer to your memo, Halloran: 'maybe' on the Dressler contract, 'no' on the Ridgewood proposal, and 'yes,' I will be your valentine."

future market growth. Either way, allocating unused capacity costs distorts estimates of the long-run, variable production costs of today's products.

Updates. A company does not need to perform the analysis and interviews for the product costing system more than once a year unless it makes major changes in its process technology, product mix, or organizational structure. Decisions regarding product introduction, abandonment, and pricing are strategic matters that should be based on the long-run marginal costs of each product.

The annual product cost computation does not have to be part of the main financial accounting system, nor does it require a lot of time and money to develop and implement. Several businesses have developed prototype product cost systems on personal computers. Of course, if a company has many products going through complex production and distribution processes, its product cost system will be more expensive to build and operate.

Even with only annual updates, managers can use the system throughout the year to influence new product design, introduction, and pricing decisions. A good system yields unit costs for all key activities (labor and machine hours, energy usage, materials, support), and it includes the unit costs of transactions like setups, shipments, part and vendor quantities, and inspections. A company can estimate a new product's cost by specifying its demands on both activities and transactions.

Including the costs of transactions like setups in product costs enhances the information given to product designers. They can better understand the costs of demands of potential products that require, for example, new components, a large number of parts, new vendors, more setups for small batch production, and more inspections for certifying tight tolerances. They can then make trade-offs among these features versus using simpler designs that exploit existing parts and vendors.

When Easy or Difficult?

One cannot generalize about the ease of designing adequate operational control and product cost systems. Companies with only a single product can estimate product costs with a trivial system. Accumulate all the expenses during a period, subtract amounts relating to future products or excess capacity, and divide the remainder by the number of units produced. Similarly, companies with continuous-flow production processes that yield homogeneous outputs can rely on measurement of product costs in units, like cost per ton or cost per gallon. Product costing for large projects like major construction, shipbuilding, or the design and manufacture of a large machine is also rather simple. In contrast, it can be extremely difficult to estimate costs of items produced by complex batch and assembly processes.

Operational control systems are simple to design and install in highly repetitive production environments, especially those governed by well-understood scientific relationships between inputs and outputs. Operational control is also easier in functional organizations where each unit performs narrowly defined functions. Furthermore, an operational control system can be installed inexpensively when production data are readily available. When product diversity is high, though, especially in production of unique items or with multiperiod production processes (as in construction, shipbuilding, and design and assembly of large, one-of-a-kind machines), operational control systems will be difficult to develop.

No single system can adequately answer the demands made by the diverse functions of cost systems. While companies can use one method to capture all their detailed transactions data, the processing of this information for diverse purposes and audiences demands separate, customized development. Companies that try to satisfy all the needs for cost information with a single system have discovered they can't perform important managerial functions adequately. Moreover, systems that work well for one company may fail in a different environment. Each company has to design methods that make sense for its particular products and processes.

The current economics of information collection, processing, and reporting have made multiple cost systems possible. Managers can exploit new trends in distributed computing by developing decentralized systems for operational control and product costing.

Of course, an argument for expanding the number of cost systems conflicts with a strongly ingrained financial culture to have only one measurement system for everyone. Eventually, designers may be smart enough to create such a system, but we don't have one today. Anytime accepted wisdom is overthrown, the world suddenly looks far more complex. When scientists declared a war on cancer more than a decade ago, for example, they thought they would need specialized cures for the hundreds of different forms of the disease. But over time and after extensive experimentation, they have begun to develop unifying theories that offer hope for more general treatments and cures.

In the same way, it is too early to discover the general system that will meet all the organization's demands for cost information. Designers must first attack the individual pieces, then with greater wisdom and insight eventually discover a general cost system that works for all managerial functions. Companies that decide to wait for such a unifying discovery, though, will suffer in the interim the consequences of using inadequate information on operating performance and product costs.

Reprint 88106

Author's note: I gratefully acknowledge the extensive contributions to this article made by my Harvard Business School colleague, Associate Professor Robin Cooper. Anthony Atkinson of Waterloo University and Ken Merchant of Harvard Business School also helped improve the presentation of key ideas.

Use activity-based costing to guide corporate strategy.

Measure Costs Right: Make the Right Decisions

by Robin Cooper and Robert S. Kaplan

Managers in companies selling multiple products are making important decisions about pricing, product mix, and process technology based on distorted cost information. What's worse, alternative information rarely exists to alert these managers that product costs are badly flawed. Most companies detect the problem only after their competitiveness and profitability have deteriorated.

Distorted cost information is the result of sensible accounting choices made decades ago, when most companies manufactured a narrow range of products. Back then, the costs of direct labor and materials, the most important production factors, could be traced easily to individual products. Distortions from allocating factory and corporate overhead by burden rates on direct labor were minor. And the expense of collecting and processing data made it hard to justify more sophisticated allocation of these and other indirect costs.

Today, product lines and marketing channels have proliferated. Direct labor now represents a small fraction of corporate costs, while expenses covering factory support operations, marketing, distribution, engineering, and other overhead functions have exploded. But most companies still allocate these rising overhead and support costs by their diminishing direct labor base or, as with marketing and distribution costs, not at all.

These simplistic approaches are no longer justifiable—especially given the plummeting costs of information technology. They can also be dangerous. Intensified global competition and radically new production technologies have made accurate product cost information crucial to competitive success.

> **Bad information on product costs leads to bad competitive strategy.**

We have written extensively on the shortcomings of typical cost accounting systems.[1] In this article we present an alternative approach, which we refer to as activity-based costing. The theory behind our method is simple. Virtually all of a company's activities exist to support the production and delivery of today's goods and services. They should therefore all be considered product costs. And since nearly all fac-

---

1. See H. Thomas Johnson and Robert S. Kaplan, *Relevance Lost: The Rise and Fall of Management Accounting* (Boston: Harvard Business School Press, 1987) and Robin Cooper and Robert S. Kaplan, "How Cost Accounting Distorts Product Costs," *Management Accounting*, April 1988, p. 20.

Robin Cooper is associate professor of business administration at the Harvard Business School and a fellow of the Institute of Chartered Accountants in England and Wales. Robert S. Kaplan is Arthur Lowes Dickinson Professor of Accounting at the Harvard Business School and professor of industrial administration at Carnegie Mellon University. This is his fourth article for HBR.

tory and corporate support costs are divisible or separable, they can be split apart and traced to individual products or product families. These costs include:

Logistics
Production
Marketing and Sales
Distribution
Service
Technology
Financial Administration
Information Resources
General Administration

Conventional economics and management accounting treat costs as variable only if they change with short-term fluctuations in output. We (and others) have found that many important cost categories vary not with short-term changes in output but with changes over a period of years in the design, mix, and range of a company's products and customers. An effective system to measure product costs must identify and assign to products these costs of complexity.

Many managers understand intuitively that their accounting systems distort product costs, so they make informal adjustments to compensate. But few can predict the magnitude and impact of the adjustments they should be making.

Consider the experience of a leading manufacturer of hydraulic valves whose product line included thousands of items. About 20% of the valves generated 80% of total revenues, a typical ratio for multiproduct organizations. Of even greater interest, 60% of the products generated 99% of the revenues. Nonetheless, management remained enthusiastic about the 40% of its products that generated only 1% of revenues. According to its cost system, these specialty items had the best gross margins.

An analysis using activity-based costing told a very different story. More than 75% of this company's products (mostly the low-volume items) were *losing* money. The products that did make money (fewer than one in four) generated more than 80% of sales and 300% of net profits.*

Top executives may be understandably reluctant to abandon existing product cost systems in favor of a new approach that reflects a radically different philosophy. We do not advocate such an abrupt overhaul. The availability of cheap, powerful personal computers, spread sheets, and data-base languages allows businesses to develop new cost systems for strate-

gic purposes off-line from official accounting systems. Companies don't have to commit their entire accounting system to activity-based costing to use it.

Indeed, activity-based costing is as much a tool of corporate strategy as it is a formal accounting system. Decisions about pricing, marketing, product design, and mix are among the most important ones managers make. None of them can be made effectively without accurate knowledge of product costs.

What Distorts Cost Data?

Product cost distortions occur in virtually all organizations producing and selling multiple products or services. To understand why, consider two hypothetical plants turning out a simple product, ballpoint pens. The factories are the same size and have the same capital equipment. Every year Plant I makes one million blue pens. Plant II also produces blue pens, but only 100,000 per year. To fill the plant, keep the work force busy, and absorb fixed costs, Plant II also produces a variety of similar products: 60,000 black pens, 12,000 red pens, 10,000 lavender pens, and so on. In a typical year, Plant II produces up to 1,000 product variations with volumes ranging between 500 and 100,000 units. Its aggregate annual output equals the one million units of Plant I, and it requires the same total standard direct labor hours, machine hours, and direct material.

Despite the similarities in product and total output, a visitor walking through the two plants would notice dramatic differences. Plant II would have a much larger production support staff — more people to schedule machines, perform setups, inspect items after setup, receive and inspect incoming materials and parts, move inventory, assemble and ship orders, expedite orders, rework defective items, design and implement engineering change orders, negotiate with vendors, schedule materials and parts receipts, and update and program the much larger computer-based information system. Plant II would also operate with considerably higher levels of idle time, overtime, inventory, rework, and scrap.

Plant II's extensive factory support resources and production inefficiencies generate cost-system distortions. Most companies allocate factory support costs in a two-step process. First, they collect the costs into categories that correspond to responsibility centers (production control, quality assurance, receiving) and assign these costs to operating departments. Many companies do this first step very well.

But the second step — tracing costs from the operating departments to specific products — is done sim-

---

* The examples in this paper of the valve manufacturer and the building supplies company were drawn from work originally done by William Boone, president of Strategic Systems Group.

plistically. Many companies still use direct labor hours as an allocation base. Others, recognizing the declining role of direct labor, use two additional allocation bases. Materials-related expenses (costs to purchase, receive, inspect, and store materials) are allocated directly to products as a percentage markup over direct materials costs. And machine hours, or processing time, are used to allocate production costs in highly automated environments.

Whether Plant II uses one or all of these approaches, its cost system invariably–and mistakenly–reports production costs for the high-volume product (blue pens) that greatly exceed the costs for the same product built in Plant I. One does not need to know much about the cost system or the production process in Plant II to predict that blue pens, which represent 10% of output, will have about 10% of the factory costs allocated to them. Similarly, lavender pens, which represent 1% of Plant II's output, will have about 1% of the factory's costs allocated to them. In fact, if the standard output per unit of direct labor hours, machine hours, and materials quantities are the same for blue pens as for lavender pens, the two types of pens will have *identical* reported costs

> Existing cost systems frequently understate profits on high-volume products and overstate profits on specialty items.

–even though lavender pens, which are ordered, fabricated, packaged, and shipped in much lower volumes, consume far more overhead per unit.

Think of the strategic consequences. Over time, the market price for blue pens, as for most high-volume products, will be determined by focused and efficient producers like Plant I. Managers of Plant II will notice that their profit margin on blue pens is lower than on their specialty products. The price for blue pens is lower than for lavender pens, but the cost system reports that blue pens are as expensive to make as the lavender.

While disappointed with the low margins on blue pens, Plant II's managers are pleased they're a full-line producer. Customers are willing to pay premiums for specialty products like lavender pens, which are apparently no more expensive to make than commodity-type blue pens. The logical strategic response? De-emphasize blue pens and offer an expanded line of differentiated products with unique features and options.

In reality, of course, this strategy will be disastrous. Blue pens in Plant II are cheaper to make than lavender pens–no matter what the cost system reports. Scaling back on blue pens and replacing the lost output by adding new models will further increase overhead. Plant II's managers will simmer with frustration as total costs rise and profitability goals remain elusive. An activity-based cost system would not generate distorted information and misguided strategic signals of this sort.

Designing an Activity-Based Cost System

The first step in designing a new product cost system is to collect accurate data on direct labor and materials costs. Next, examine the demands made by particular products on indirect resources. Three rules should guide this process:

1. Focus on expensive resources.
2. Emphasize resources whose consumption varies significantly by product and product type; look for diversity.
3. Focus on resources whose demand patterns are uncorrelated with traditional allocation measures like direct labor, processing time, and materials.

Rule 1 leads us to resource categories where the new costing process has the potential to make big differences in product costs. A company that makes industrial goods with a high ratio of factory costs to total costs will want a system that emphasizes tracing manufacturing overhead to products. A consumer goods producer will want to analyze its marketing, distribution, and service costs by product lines, channels, customers, and regions. High-technology companies must study the demands made on engineering, product improvement, and process development resources by their different products and product lines.

Rules 2 and 3 identify resources with the greatest potential for distortion under traditional systems. They point to activities for which the usual surrogates–labor hours, material quantities, or machine hours–do not represent adequate measures of resource consumption. The central question is, which parts of the organization tend to grow as the company increases the diversity of its product line, its processing technologies, its customer base, its marketing channels, its supplier base?

The process of tracing costs, first from resources to activities and then from activities to specific products, cannot be done with surgical precision. We cannot estimate to four significant digits the added

Allocating Costs under an Activity-Based System

The process of designing and implementing an activity-based cost system for support departments usually begins with interviews of the department heads. The interviews yield insights into departmental operations and into the factors that trigger departmental activities. Subsequent analysis traces these activities to specific products.

The following example illustrates the activity-based costing process for an inventory control department responsible for raw materials and purchased components. The annual costs associated with the department (mainly personnel costs) are $500,000.

Interview Department Head

Q: How many people work for you?
A: Twelve.

Q: What do they do?
A: Six of them spend most of their time handling incoming shipments of purchased parts. They handle everything—from documentation to transferring parts to the WIP stockroom. Three others work in raw materials. After the material clears inspection, they move it into inventory and take care of the paperwork.

Q: What determines the time required to process an incoming shipment? Does it matter if the shipment is large or small?
A: Not for parts. They go directly to the WIP stockroom, and unless it's an extremely large shipment it can be handled in one trip. With raw materials, though, volume can play a big role in processing time. But there are only a few large raw material shipments. Over the course of a year, the time required to process a part or raw material really depends on the number of times it's received, not on the size of the shipments in which it comes.

Q: What other factors affect your department's work load?
A: Well, there are three people I haven't discussed yet. They disburse raw material to the shop floor. Again, volume is not really an issue; it's more the number of times material has to be disbursed.

Q: Do you usually disburse the total amount of material required for a production run all at once, or does it go out in smaller quantities?
A: It varies with the size of the run. On a big run we can't disburse it all at once—there would be too much raw material on the shop floor. On smaller runs—and I'd say that's 80% of all runs—we'd send it there in a single trip once setup is complete.

Design the System

After the interview, the system designer can use the number of people involved in each activity to allocate the department's $500,000 cost:

Activity	People	Total Cost
Receiving purchased parts	6	$250,000
Receiving raw material	3	$125,000
Disbursing material	3	$125,000

In 1987, this company received 25,000 shipments of purchased parts and 10,000 shipments of raw materials. The factory made 5,000 production runs. Dividing these totals into the support dollars associated with each activity yields the following costs per unit of activity:

Activity	Allocation Measure	Unit Cost
Receiving purchased parts	Number of shipments per year	$10 per shipment
Receiving raw material	Number of shipments per year	$12.50 per shipment
Disbursing material	Number of production runs	$25 per run

We can now attribute inventory control support costs to specific products. Suppose the company manufactures 1,000 units of Product A in a year. Product A is a complex product with more than 50 purchased parts and several different types of raw material. During the year, the 1,000 units were assembled in 10 different production runs requiring 200 purchased parts shipments and 50 different raw material shipments. Product A incurs $2,875 in inventory control overhead ($10 × 200 + $12.50 × 50 + $25 × 10) to produce the 1,000 units, or $2.88 of inventory control costs per unit.

Product A also consumed 1,000 hours of direct labor out of the factory's total of 400,000 hours. A labor-based allocation system would allocate $1,250 of inventory control costs to the 1,000 units produced ($500,000/400,000 × 1,000) for a per-unit cost of $1.25. The 230% cost difference between the activity-based attribution ($2.88) and the labor-based allocation ($1.25) reflects the fact that the complex, low-volume Product A demands a much greater share of inventory control resources than its share of factory direct-labor hours.

burden on support resources of introducing two new variations of a product. But it is better to be basically correct with activity-based costing, say, within 5% or 10% of the actual demands a product makes on organizational resources, than to be precisely wrong (perhaps by as much as 200%) using outdated allocation techniques.

The insert "Allocating Costs under an Activity-Based System" shows how a company might calculate and assign the support costs of a common manufacturing overhead function–raw materials and parts control. The principles and methods, while illustrated in a conventional manufacturing setting, are applicable to any significant collection of corporate resources in the manufacturing or service sector.

The Impact of Activity-Based Costing

An activity-based system can paint a picture of product costs radically different from data generated by traditional systems. These differences arise because of the system's more sophisticated approach to attributing factory overhead, corporate overhead, and other organizational resources, first to activities and then to the products that create demand for these indirect resources.

Manufacturing Overhead. Let's look more closely at the manufacturer of hydraulic valves mentioned earlier. Cost information on seven representative products is presented in the table "How Activity-Based Costing Changes Product Profitability." Under the old cost system, the overhead charge per unit did not differ much among the seven valves, ranging from $5.34 to $8.88. Under the new system, which traces overhead costs directly to factory support activities and then to products, the range in overhead cost per unit widened dramatically–from $4.39 to $77.64. With four low- to medium-volume products (valves 2 through 5), the overhead cost estimate increased by 100% or more. For the two highest volume products (valves 1 and 6), the overhead cost declined.

The strategic consequences of these data are enormous. Under the labor-based cost system, valve 3 was considered the most profitable product of the seven, with a gross margin of 47%. The activity-based system, in contrast, revealed that when orders for valve 3 arrived, the company would have done better to mail its customers cash to buy the valves elsewhere than to make them itself.

Labor-based cost systems don't always underestimate the overhead demands of low-volume products.

Valve 7, with the second lowest volume in the group, shows a marked decrease in overhead under an activity-based system. Why? Valve 7 is assembled from components already being used on the high-volume products (valves 1 and 6). The bulk of any factory's overhead costs are associated with ordering parts, keeping track of them, inspecting them, and setting up to produce components. For parts and components ordered or fabricated in large volumes, the per-unit impact of these transaction costs is modest. Therefore, specialized products assembled from high-volume components will have low production costs even if shipping volume is not high.

Marketing Expenses. The redesign of cost systems should not be limited to factory support costs. Many companies have selling, general, and administrative (SG&A) expenses that exceed 20% of total revenues. Yet they treat these costs as period expenses, not charges to be allocated to products. While such "below the [gross margin] line" treatment may be adequate, even required, for financial accounting, it is poor practice for measuring product costs.

We studied a building supplies company that distributed its products through six channels–two in the consumer market and four in the commercial market. Across all its products, this company had an average gross margin of 34%. Marketing costs for the six channels averaged 16.4% of sales, with general and administrative expenses another 8.5%. (The tables entitled "OEM Changes from a Laggard...to a Solid Performer" present information on the four commercial channels.)

With operating profits in the commercial sector at only about 10% of revenues, the company was look-

> Management thought valve 3 was a cash cow. It might as well have mailed checks to its customers.

ing to improve its profitability. Management decided to focus on SG&A expenses. Previously, the company had allocated SG&A costs by assigning 25% of sales –the company average–to each distribution segment. A more sophisticated analysis, similar in philosophy to the overhead analysis performed by the hydraulic valve company, produced striking changes in product costs.

The OEM business was originally a prime target for elimination. Its 27% gross margin and laggard 2% operating margin put it at the bottom of the pack among commercial channels. But the OEM channel

How Activity-Based Costing Changes Product Profitability*

Valve Number	Annual Volume (units)	Manufacturing Overhead Per Unit			Gross Margin	
		Old System	New System	Percent Difference	Old System	New System
1	43,562	$5.44	$ 4.76	− 12.5%	41%	46%
2	500	6.15	12.86	+109.0	30	− 24
3	53	7.30	77.64	+964.0	47	−258
4	2,079	8.88	19.76	+123.0	26	− 32
5	5,670	7.58	15.17	+100.0	39	2
6	11,196	5.34	5.26	− 1.5	41	41
7	423	5.92	4.39	− 26.0	31	43

*We are not confident that the table's figures are exactly correct. For example, students of this case have estimated the appropriate overhead charge on valve 3 (listed at $77.64 per unit) to be as low as $64 and as high as $84. Whatever the exact figure, the difference between this activity-based cost and the original estimate ($7.30 per unit) suggests that the current labor-based system is seriously flawed.

used virtually no resources in several major selling categories: advertising, catalog, sales promotion, and warranty. In the remaining selling categories, the OEM channel used proportionately fewer resources per sales dollar than the other major channels. Its marketing expenses were 9% of sales, well below the 15% average for the four commercial channels. A sounder estimate of OEM operating margin was 9%, not 2%.

The OEM segment looked even better after the company extended the analysis by allocating invested capital to specific channels. The OEM business required far less investment in working capital—accounts receivable and inventory—than the other commercial channels. Thus, even though the OEM channel had a below-average gross margin, its bottom-line return-on-investment turned out to be higher than the commercial average.

Other Corporate Overhead. Virtually all organizational costs, not just factory overhead or marketing expenses, can and should be traced to the activities for which these resources are used, and then to the divisions, channels, and product lines that consume them. Weyerhaeuser Company recently instituted a charge-back system to trace corporate overhead department costs to the activities that drive them.[2]

For example, Weyerhaeuser's financial services department analyzed all the activities it performed—including data-base administration, general accounting, accounts payable and receivable, and invoicing—to determine what factors create demands for them. A division dealing with a small number of high-volume customers makes very different demands on activities like accounts receivable from a division with many low-volume customers. Before instituting the charge-back system, Weyerhaeuser applied the cost of accounts receivable and other functions as a uniform percentage of a division's sales—a driver that bore little or no relation to the activities that created the administrative work. Now it allocates costs based on which divisions (and product lines) generate the costs.

Similarly, companies engaged in major product development and process improvements should attribute the costs of design and engineering resources to the products and product lines that benefit from them. Otherwise, product and process modification costs will be shifted onto product lines for which little development effort is being performed.

Where Does Activity-Based Costing Stop?

We believe that only two types of costs should be excluded from a system of activity-based costing. First, the costs of excess capacity should not be charged to individual products. To use a simplified example, consider a one-product plant whose practical production capacity is one million units per year. The plant's total annual costs amount to $5 million. At full capacity the cost per unit is $5. This is the unit product cost the company should use regardless of the plant's budgeted production volume. The cost of excess or idle capacity should be treated as a separate line item—a cost of the period, not of individual products.

2. See H. Thomas Johnson and Dennis A. Loewe, "How Weyerhaeuser Manages Corporate Overhead Costs," *Management Accounting*, August 1987, p. 20.

OEM Changes from a Laggard...
Profits by Commercial Distribution Channel (Old System)

	Contract	Industrial Suppliers	Government	OEM	Total Commercial
Annual Sales *(in thousands of dollars)*	$79,434	$25,110	$422	$9,200	$114,166
Gross Margin	34%	41%	23%	27%	35%
Gross Profit	$27,375	$10,284	$136	$2,461	$ 40,256
SG&A Allowance* *(in thousands of dollars)*	$19,746	$ 6,242	$105	$2,287	$ 31,814
Operating Profit *(in thousands of dollars)*	$ 7,629	$ 4,042	$ 31	$ 174	$ 11,876
Operating Margin	10%	16%	7%	2%	10%
Invested Capital Allowance† *(in thousands of dollars)*	$33,609	$10,624	$179	$3,893	$ 48,305
Return on Investment	23%	38%	17%	4%	25%

*SG&A allowance for each channel is 25% of that channel's revenues.
†Invested capital allowance for each channel is 42% of that channel's revenues.

Many companies, however, spread capacity costs over budgeted volume. Returning to our example, if demand exists for only 500,000 units, a traditional cost system will report that each unit cost $10 to build ($5 million/500,000) even though workers and machines have become no less efficient in terms of what they could produce. Such a procedure causes product costs to fluctuate erratically with changes in assumed production volume and can lead to the "death spiral." A downturn in forecast demand creates idle capacity. The cost system reports higher costs. So management raises prices, which guarantees even less demand in the future and still higher idle capacity costs.

The second exclusion from an activity-based cost system is research and development for entirely new products and lines. We recommend splitting R&D costs into two categories: those that relate to improvements and modifications of existing products and lines and those that relate to entirely new products. The first category can and should be traced to the products that will benefit from the development effort. Otherwise, the costs will be spread to products and lines that bear no relationship to the applied R&D program.

The second category is a different animal. Financial accounting treats R&D as a cost of the period in which it takes place. The management accounting system, in contrast, should treat these costs as investments in the future. Companies engaged in extensive R&D for products with short life cycles should measure costs and revenues over the life cycle of their products. Any periodic assessment of product profitability will be misleading, since it depends on the arbitrary amortization of investment expenditures including R&D.

Strategic Implications

The examples we've discussed demonstrate how an activity-based cost system can lead to radically different evaluations of product costs and profitability than more simplistic approaches. It does not imply that because some low-volume products (lavender pens or valve 3) now are unprofitable, a company should immediately drop them. Many customers value having a single source of supply, a big reason companies become full-line producers. It may be impossible to cherry pick a line and build only profitable products. If the multiproduct pen company wants to sell its profitable blue and black pens, it may have to absorb the costs of filling the occasional order for lavender pens.

Once executives are armed with more reliable cost information, they can ponder a range of strategic options. Dropping unprofitable products is one. So is raising prices, perhaps drastically. Many low-volume products have surprisingly low price elasticities. Customers who want lavender pens or valve 3 may be willing to pay much more than the current price. On the other hand, these customers may also react to a price increase by switching away from low-volume products. That too is acceptable; the company would be supplying fewer money-losing items.

...to a Solid Performer
Profits by Commercial Distribution Channel (New System)

	Contract	Industrial Suppliers	Government	OEM	Total Commercial
Gross Profit *(from previous table)*	$27,375	$10,284	$136	$2,461	$40,256
Selling Expenses* *(all in thousands of dollars)*					
Commission	$ 4,682	$ 1,344	$ 12	$ 372	$ 6,410
Advertising	132	38	0	2	172
Catalog	504	160	0	0	664
Co-op Advertising	416	120	0	0	536
Sales Promotion	394	114	0	2	510
Warranty	64	22	0	4	90
Sales Administration	5,696	1,714	20	351	7,781
Cash Discount	892	252	12	114	1,270
Total	$12,780	$ 3,764	$ 44	$ 845	$17,433
G&A *(in thousands of dollars)*	$ 6,740	$ 2,131	$ 36	$ 781	$ 9,688
Operating Profit *(in thousands of dollars)*	$ 7,855	$ 4,389	$ 56	$ 835	$13,135
Operating Margin	10%	17%	13%	9%	12%
Invested Capital*	$33,154	$10,974	$184	$2,748	$47,060
Return on Investment	24%	40%	30%	30%	28%

*Selling expenses and invested capital estimated under an activity-based system.

More accurate cost information also raises strategic options for high-volume products. Plant II might consider dropping its prices on blue pens. The old cost system, which shifted overhead charges onto these high-volume products, created a price umbrella that benefited focused competitors like Plant I. Pricing its core product more competitively might help Plant II reverse a market-share slide.

Managers in the building supplies company we described took several profit-enhancing steps after receiving the revised cost data by distribution channels. They began emphasizing the newly attractive OEM segment and any new business where marketing costs would be well below the company average.

Information generated by an activity-based cost system can also encourage companies to redesign products to use more common parts. Managers frequently exhort their engineers to design or modify products so they use fewer parts and are easier to manufacture. But these exhortations will ring hollow if the company's cost system cannot identify the benefits to design and manufacturing simplicity. Recall valve 7, a low-volume product made from components fabricated in large volumes for other products. Now that the company can quantify, using activity-based techniques, the impressive cost bene-

fits of component standardization, the entire organization will better understand the value of designing products for manufacturability.

Likewise, activity-based costing can change how managers evaluate new process technologies. Streamlining the manufacturing process to reduce setup times, rationalizing plant layout to lower material handling costs, and improving quality to reduce postproduction inspections can all have major impacts on product costs—impacts that become visible on a product-by-product basis with activity-based costing. A more accurate understanding of the costs of specialized products may also make computer-integrated manufacturing (CIM) look more attractive, since CIM is most efficient in high-variety, low-volume environments.

Activity-based costing is not designed to trigger automatic decisions. It is designed to provide more accurate information about production and support activities and product costs so that management can focus its attention on the products and processes with the most leverage for increasing profits. It helps managers make better decisions about product design, pricing, marketing, and mix, and encourages continual operating improvements.

Reprint 88503

How Hewlett-Packard Gets Numbers It Can Trust

by Debbie Berlant, Reese Browning, and George Foster

Five years ago, people at the Roseville Networks Division of Hewlett-Packard didn't believe the numbers the accounting system produced. Now they do. When marketing, manufacturing, product design, and accounting sat down to discuss a product, we invariably argued about how to find a product's "real" cost. Production, in particular, viewed accounting as a watchdog, not a fellow decision maker. We no longer have those arguments. Today production and accounting jointly make decisions that meet everyone's needs.

What's changed is the accounting system. Over the past five years, largely in response to fundamental changes in manufacturing, Roseville Networks Division (RND) has developed a new accounting system that measures the factors that truly drive costs. The cost-driver or activity-based system is more accurate, more timely, and ultimately more useful to its "customers" – the manufacturing, R&D, and marketing people who rely on the information it provides.

We're still improving our accounting system, but the results so far have been profoundly positive. In fact, RND has been held up as a model for other Hewlett-Packard organizations, and the computer-manufacturing division, which is a level above us, has mandated that all its manufacturing organizations use a cost-driver accounting system based on ours. Accurate and timely cost information is imperative in the highly competitive computer market. We can now provide it.

Mavericks of accounting

RND is a low-volume, high-mix factory. It makes about 250 products (mostly printed-circuit assemblies and mechanical devices for use with central-processing units), each of which has various options – for a total of about 1,100 different items. Sometime in the early 1980s, RND's manufacturing manager took a tour of factories in Japan. He came back with a vision. His observations of Japanese production techniques had inspired him to transform RND's manufacturing into a process environment. That is, he wanted to change the plant's focus from individual products to manufacturing processes. He wanted to be able to send any of those 1,100 items down the line, one at a time, in a continuous flow uninterrupted by setup or configuration changes.

The manufacturing manager enlisted the help of six people – from manufacturing, finance, and information systems – to implement his vision. He explained that their mission was to understand a process, document it, simplify it, and automate it if necessary. He encouraged this "Simple Six" task force to question everything, and it did.

The team scrutinized every existing procedure, even the measurements manufacturing was making. When assembly workers manually inserted parts on circuit boards, for instance, they had to note how much time they spent on the task. When technicians conducted a test, they had to track the time spent and voucher this time to a specified work order. Manufacturing used some of the measurements to monitor costs for its own purposes, but it tracked other things simply because the accounting system needed the data. The designers, too, gathered some data simply to satisfy accounting and used other information to estimate product costs for themselves.

These private accounting systems were a strong indication that the ac-

Debbie Berlant, cost accounting supervisor at Hewlett-Packard's Roseville Networks Division, and Reese Browning, cost accounting manager also at RND, helped develop and implement the division's cost-driver accounting system. George Foster, the Paul L. and Phyllis Wattis Professor of Accounting at Stanford University's Graduate School of Business, has examined the competitive advantages of Hewlett-Packard's and other companies' cost management systems.

counting system was not giving customers information they trusted. We had heard complaints about the accounting system before, often at meetings that involved people from different functions. When we costed a new product, for instance, marketing, manufacturing, product design, and accounting each came up with a different number. Arguments inevitably ensued about which number was right but also about the method used to arrive at it. The problem for many people was that regardless of how they calculated costs in their own departments, the numbers from the official accounting system were the ones that stuck.

We in accounting were aware of people's complaints, but the Simple Six's drive to eliminate unnecessary measurements was the real impetus to rethink our internal cost accounting system. And we had to adjust to the changes in manufacturing anyway.

Accountants tend to be pretty conservative and to view the company narrowly. We were lucky to have had a cost accounting manager who was

> Why did manufacturing, marketing, and design arrive at different costs for the same product?

something of a maverick. He was willing to redesign the accounting system to give manufacturing the information it needed and to eliminate the record keeping it found burdensome – as long as the system continued to meet accounting's needs. We still had to ensure the integrity of the data for GAAP, set standard costs, track actuals against standards, verify and value inventory, and determine our sales discounts and cost of sales.

We spent a lot of time thinking about what a cost system should do. We needed it for valuing inventory,

for cost control and performance measurement, and for decision making and designing for manufacturability. After discussing the possibility of creating a separate cost system for each of these functions, we decided that one system could in fact provide all the numbers that we needed.

The goal for accounting, then, was to design one system that would accurately reflect manufacturing costs, use data that manufacturing could collect easily, and meet the legal and practical needs of the accounting function.

What manufacturing taught accounting

We can trace our new cost accounting system to a conversation we had with the production manager. We had costed a new product with our usual accounting numbers, and the production manager hotly disagreed with the result. He understood the manufacturing processes well and knew that the product didn't require a lot of complicated procedures. He couldn't believe the product cost as much as we said it did. When we went into the plant to discuss the matter, he sat down at his PC. Here was manufacturing's private accounting system, which was to become the seed of our new, official accounting system.

Every printed circuit board RND makes has diodes, capacitors, and integrated circuits inserted on it. The boards begin at a "start station," where instructions for building the board are entered into a computer. The software then tells the automated equipment what parts to insert where. Diodes and capacitors are inserted by a process called axial insertion; integrated circuits, by dip insertion; certain other components, by hand.

The boards move from the start station to auto insertion and on through a wave-solder machine. From there, they go into "backloading," or final assembly, where parts that cannot be wave soldered are attached and soldered by hand. Completed boards then move to a test station, and, if they fail, to a troubleshooting station.

The production manager took the total amount expected to be spent on the start station and various kinds of insertions and divided it by the number of circuit boards that went through those processes. If the total annual cost was, say, $130,500, and 145,000 insertions were made, he said each insertion should cost 90 cents ($130,500 divided by 145,000).

Our old accounting system lumped the overhead cost of the start station and auto insertion into one bucket and applied it across products (in the controller's words, "like peanut butter") based on how much direct labor time they required. With manufacturing overhead some 30% of a product's total cost, it made sense to better understand how products really used the things it included. Manufacturing's alternative cost system was definitely a step in the right direction. It tried to allocate costs according to the things that were really driving them.

RND's traditional internal accounting system served us well for years. It had the usual three categories of costs – direct material, direct labor, and manufacturing overhead. In the early 1980s, following the recommendations of a corporatewide study, we improved the system by dividing manufacturing overhead into three separate cost pools: procurement overhead, production overhead, and support overhead.

Procurement overhead included the costs of buying materials and of receiving, storing, handling, and documenting them. It was assigned to products based on material dollars. Production overhead included the cost of activities required to assemble and test products and was allocated by direct labor hours. Support overhead included production engineering, central data-processing support, process engineering, and manufacturing management. It was allocated to the other two categories of overhead before they were, in turn, allocated to material and labor.

But people complained about the system, even after improvements. Procurement said that allocating procurement overhead to products according to material dollars made no sense. Our parts are fairly small, and their costs vary widely. But while some parts cost much less than others, they require approximately the same effort when it comes to buying, documenting, handling, storing, and cycle counting them. The overhead allocated to inexpensive parts didn't reflect the real cost of procuring and handling them.

The product designers had a different concern. They said the overhead that was attached to each dollar of direct labor created an incentive to design direct labor out of the products, even when the alternative design would be harder to manufacture. Meanwhile, the production people complained that direct labor hours had little to do with how many manufacturing resources a product really consumed. And marketing complained that commodity-type products were too expensive and blamed the accounting system for systematically overcosting them.

The production manager had the right idea. Finding what really drives costs became the key to making our new accounting system more useful and accurate.

Creating the system

Our new accounting system started as a very simple model, partly because conventional wisdom says it's hard for people to accept a new system if it's complicated and partly because we wanted to implement the system quickly. We tested a prototype in 1984, and a year later, we gathered up our courage to launch it as the primary internal accounting system. We have been refining it—adding sophistication—ever since. As it turns out, no one minds greater sophistication as long as it makes the system better.

Designing the new system required a number of big decisions. First, we had to specify which costs to trace directly to individual products. We initially decided to stick with the categories we had: direct labor, direct material, and overhead. In 1986, we eliminated the direct labor category altogether by combining it with overhead. That was a bold step for us, but it made sense.

For RND, as for many manufacturing companies, direct labor had shrunk to a very small portion of total product costs. The year we finally eliminated direct labor, it was averaging less than 2% of total

> **We used to spend half an hour a day tracking direct labor. Now we lump it into overhead.**

manufacturing costs. Yet we were spending a lot of time tracking it. We estimated that 30 minutes of direct labor time per person each day was spent on vouchering labor time directly to individual products.

We started asking ourselves why we were measuring labor when we knew that it was no different from depreciation—it was a cost of the process. But we weren't sure we could just drop it altogether. We knew of no one else in the company that had. So we asked some questions and eventually got corporate approval to stop reporting it. Of course, we didn't actually eliminate the cost; we just pooled it with our overhead. Unless it's working on a nonproduction activity such as pilot runs for the lab, accounting doesn't require production to voucher its time anymore.

We also had to decide on the categories of manufacturing overhead costs. We retained the three subcategories of the old system: procurement overhead, production overhead, and support overhead, which is allocated to the first two categories.

Within these categories, we had to separate the important activities. To start, we defined them broadly. Manufacturing's private cost system lumped the start station and the various kinds of automated insertions together, for example, so we did too. It grouped wave solder and final assembly; so did we.

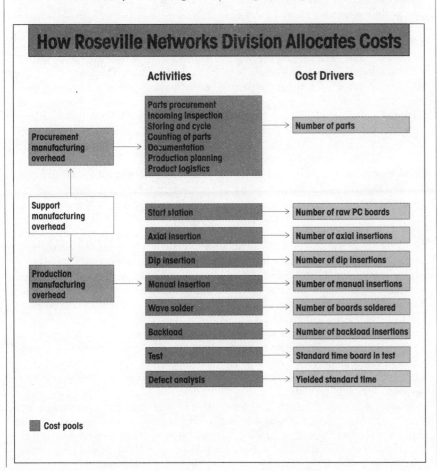

How Roseville Networks Division Allocates Costs

Activities	Cost Drivers
Parts procurement / Incoming inspection / Storing and cycle Counting of parts / Documentation / Production planning / Product logistics	Number of parts
Start station	Number of raw PC boards
Axial insertion	Number of axial insertions
Dip insertion	Number of dip insertions
Manual insertion	Number of manual insertions
Wave solder	Number of boards soldered
Backload	Number of backload insertions
Test	Standard time board in test
Defect analysis	Yielded standard time

Procurement manufacturing overhead → (parts activities)
Support manufacturing overhead
Production manufacturing overhead → (production activities)

■ Cost pools

How Roseville Networks Division Costs a PC Board

Product Cost of PC Board Type 67

Direct materials	$ 75.17
Procurement overhead	9.40
Production overhead	38.07
	122.64

Procurement Overhead Cost

Procurement:	94 parts	×	$ .10 each	=	$ 9.40

Production Overhead Cost

Start station:	1 raw PC Board	×	$ .90 each	=	$ .90
Axial insertion:	43 axial insertions	×	.06 each	=	2.58
Dip insertion:	30 dip insertions	×	.17 each	=	5.10
Manual insertion:	13 manual insertions	×	.35 each	=	4.55
Wave solder:	1 board soldered	×	2.50 each	=	2.50
Backload:	6 backload insertions	×	.58 each	=	3.48
Test:	.20 hours board is in test process	×	70.00 per hour	=	14.00
Defect analysis:	.08 hours for defect analysis and repair	×	62.00 per hour	=	4.96
					$38.07

As we used the system, people in the labs and in production wanted activities defined more narrowly. When we set standard costs on one particular new product, for example, the design engineer was shocked. He didn't believe the product could cost that much. He explained that the product used only axial components, which are much less expensive to insert than dip components, and urged us to differentiate between the two processes. We calmed him down and took a look at the situation. He was right. There was about a three-to-one difference in cost.

We had also grouped together wave solder and final assembly, but the only information we were capturing was whether a circuit board went through final assembly. If it didn't, then it wasn't charged for wave solder either. Yet every board was going across the wave-solder machine. When production pointed out the problem, we broke the activities apart.

We now list seven activities in the procurement overhead category and eight activities in production overhead. We combine the costs of the seven in procurement because they all have the same cost driver, but we separate the costs of each of the eight production activities because of differing drivers. (See the chart, "How RND Allocates Costs.")

The last step in designing the system was determining what was driving costs for the various activities. This may sound hard, but it was really just a matter of talking to the people on the factory floor. The drivers were usually obvious to them. Take axial insertion. What does an axial insertion machine do? It inserts. Therefore, the driver is the number of axial insertions.

When we separated wave solder from final assembly, we had trouble deciding what the wave-solder cost driver was. The number of holes? The number of leads on a board? The number of components? Any of these measures would probably have worked, but there was no easy way of capturing that information systematically. We finally decided to charge a flat rate per assembly. Even if we were off by 50%, which wasn't likely since our products are all about the same size, the absolute dollars wouldn't distort product costs.

In the old system, we had been using standard time to allocate the cost of product-verification testing. We

thought it would be simpler to use a flat rate. Soon afterward, though, we came to understand how very different the tests are, and we ended up going back to the original driver, standard time.

In final assembly, manufacturing wanted to send the design lab a message about the insertion of jumper wires, a step that was manual-intensive and difficult. They insisted that the accounting system was burying the cost and wanted us to isolate it. When we did, we discovered that inserting jumper wires cost roughly $7.50 – an expense designers would go out of their way to avoid.

We recognize that costs cannot be traced with surgical precision. But we're convinced that at least for now, we have found cost drivers that produce more accurate product costs than before. (See the exhibit, "How RND Costs a PC Board," for a fictionalized example of how RND's new system works.)

Getting physical

The new accounting system has had a number of unexpected and important results. For one thing, it allows people to think in more physical terms – which is how engineers and designers like to think anyway. When we were allocating some 30% of costs by direct labor, which itself was just 2% of costs, it was hard to see what exactly was contributing to a product's cost. Now we see that the process of physically assembling a product uses resources. We understand that it costs a dollar and some change for a board to go through the start station because we can see the activity. And we understand that every time the axial insertion machine "kerchunks," it costs something.

Engineers, designers, and accountants still argue – but over different things. We may dispute whether something should cost more or less, but how the costs come together is no longer an issue. We speak the same language, and the emotionalism is gone. Even the very precise lab engineers who may not accept the exactness of the cost-driver rates believe that the relative differences help them make sensible trade-offs between different types of components and processes.

The people who use the system continue to propose ways to improve it. Manufacturing has pointed out that certain things the system now treats as homogeneous actually have costs that are different enough to warrant creating separate cost pools for them. For instance, radial insertions are still lumped together with the more costly axial insertions. Similarly, manual insertion and masking (taping components that cannot be wave soldered) are combined, as are royonics, mechanical assembly, and hand soldering.

Another improvement we are considering is incorporating volume-sensitive cost relationships. Setting up the dip insertion machine always costs the same, regardless of how many parts are being produced, yet right now we don't account for that. We may decide to establish a fixed cost for setup, which would of course raise the reported cost of low-volume components. Managers will have the option of substituting a different operation for low-volume parts.

Our purchasing managers have suggested ways to make costs more accurately reflect the resources they spend on procurement – by adjusting for order volume, prior relationships with vendors, and the amount of testing purchased parts require. One proposed scheme for dealing with order size is to vary the flat rate charge per item depending on the total quantity of the order. An order for 50 parts would incur a procurement overhead cost of $1 per part, for example, while an order of more than a million would cost just 4 cents per part.

We in accounting take the feedback we get from line people in various functions as a good sign. It shows that they're committed to the cost system and interested in helping us refine it. We have succeeded in creating an accounting system that focuses primarily on the cost of a process. Attaching that cost to a product is a secondary – albeit necessary – task. One product designer said it best: "Finally, we have numbers we can have some faith in."

Reprint 90104

*Knowing your real profit economics is
key to staying competitive.*

Vital Truths About Managing Your Costs

by B. Charles Ames and James D. Hlavacek

Few truisms apply universally in the business world, but four related ones are valid in every business situation.

1. Over the long term, it is absolutely essential to be a lower cost supplier.

2. To stay competitive, inflation-adjusted costs of producing and supplying any product or service must continuously trend downward.

3. The true cost and profit picture for each product, for each product/market segment, and for all key customers must always be known, and traditional accounting practices must not obscure them.

4. A business must concentrate on cash flow and balance-sheet strengths as much as on profits.

B. Charles Ames is chairman and CEO of Uniroyal Goodrich Tire Company and a partner at Clayton & Dubilier, Inc. James D. Hlavacek is managing director of a Charlotte-based management training and consulting firm and is professor of management, on leave, at Wake Forest University. The authors' book, Market Driven Management: Prescriptions for Surviving in a Turbulent World *(Dow Jones-Irwin), was published last year.*

These truths are more important than ever because there is increasingly less margin for error in our increasingly more competitive global business environment.

The Lower Cost Supplier

No company, whether industrial, high-tech, or service, can succeed over the long term unless it is a lower cost supplier than all others providing equivalent products or services. Short-term survival might be possible but not long-term success. Proprietary advantage never lasts. Maturity and decline come to products and businesses as they do to life, and prices and margins inevitably succumb to pressures. As competitive product distinctions fade, price becomes increasingly important in buying decisions. The more effective suppliers will constantly improve productivity and reduce costs. Thus, even when price pressures get intense, margins will at least be maintained. When this is not done, profits and market position almost certainly fall. Summarizing retrospectively, Paul Allaire, president of Xerox, told a reporter in 1988, "Until the mid-1970s, we were the undisputed copier king. [Finally] we realized the Japanese were selling quality products for what it cost us to make them. We learned the hard way how quickly our competition can turn market supremacy into market oblivion."

Being a lower cost supplier doesn't necessarily mean being lowest cost among all competitors. Nor does it mean that you can't or shouldn't have a strategy of producing at a higher cost and selling at a

Costs don't mean just production costs; overhead and other costs can throw your total cost structure out of line.

higher price. But it does mean that one's total costs should be well below the average of all competitors offering equivalent products or services to the same customer segments.

Costs don't mean just production costs. Overhead or other costs like designing, selling, delivering, or servicing can throw the total cost structure out of line. These tend to overaccumulate in good times when there's no pressure for tight performance and common sense.

Inflation is another enemy of sense and effectiveness. In the late 1970s and early 1980s, it provided a cushion that allowed companies to avoid addressing their costs properly. It was easy to raise prices when costs went up, because demand was bullish and often exceeded supplier capacity. Situations like this lead to indiscipline. The health care industry is a good example. For 20 years, it was a cost-plus reimbursement industry where prices were allowed to ride up with unmanaged costs. When third-party payers (government and insurance companies) and then employers finally came to their senses, a lot of health care providers that had let costs go uncontrolled got into trouble. Abbott Laboratories escaped that fate. In an interview last year, its longtime Chairman and CEO Robert Schoellhorn, decreed:

"To simply raise prices along with the industry is not the Abbott way. Our overall corporate measure of productivity is sales per employee. Price increases don't get factored in. Paying close attention to such things as head count becomes second nature. You must develop an attitude throughout the company that you can always find a better and lower cost way to do things. Our constant effort to lower unit costs also makes more money available for new products

and for price-cutting assaults. They help keep old competitors at bay and new ones away."

Logic suggests that, over time, the real, inflation-adjusted costs of doing business should be downward—because as organizations learn how to do things better, they also get more efficient. This is the underlying principle of the experience curve, and it really works: from 1981 to 1989, the computer hardware cost of processing a million instructions per second dropped 76% for mainframes, 86% for minicomputers, and 93% for PCs. In color-film processing, a 3"x5" print fell from 50 cents for 5-day service in 1970 to 20 cents for 1-day service in 1984. In the manufacturing of power hand tools, the cost fell 29% with each doubling of output between 1965 to 1984. And in the low-value-added category of broken and crushed limestone, costs fell about 25% over the 30-year period ending in 1973.

But these continual cost reductions did not come automatically with experience or the passage of time. They required constant management attentiveness in all matters to continuing productivity gains and cost reductions. Too often products and costs drift out of competitive line, and no one realizes it until it is too late. Managers who claim that they are a lower or even the lowest cost producer rarely

Isolate your costs and assign them to specific products, accounts, or markets.

know what their true costs are or how they compare with competitors'. Even when there is clear evidence that competitors are selling at a lower price, many managers will deny any kind of a cost disadvantage. Instead they will say that their competitors are "stupid" or "aren't as concerned about profits as we are."

To know exactly what your costs are and to manage them well, you must carefully isolate various costs and assign them to specific products, accounts, or markets. Such assignments are often done badly. The most common mistake is to work on the basis of "average" costs, as if all costs were equally shared by all products and customers. Average costing ignores important differences among products and the fact that different products, different markets, and different customers incur different overhead costs. The broader the product line, the more distortions result from cost averaging, which nearly always leads to "average" price increases or decreases. In average pricing, some products or customers are overcharged while others are subsidized. Across-the-board price changes ignore true product-line cost differences and differences in customer price sensitivities. Average costing that results in average price changes can lead to a loss of profit, reduced volume, declining market share, and the dulling of management spirit.

What All This Means

No company can be successful over time if inflation-adjusted total costs do not follow a steadily declining pattern.

Management must place unrelenting pressure on the entire organization for measurable cost reductions and productivity gains, year after year. The rate of improvement may vary annually but should never fall below inflation. Vigilance is critical because it is so difficult to regain cost competitiveness once it has been lost. Costs should not be allowed to get out of line in the first place.

Companies should add large increments of capacity grudgingly, especially as the business matures, but even in growing businesses. In today's fast-moving world, life cycles are shorter and payback cycles must be shorter. Furthermore, companies should evaluate capital appropriations against profits from the least profitable part of the business, since they can always drop the less profitable parts or not make the contemplated addition or both.

If your costs have become noncompetitive, then probably traditional expense reductions alone – cutting back here and there, reducing overhead, saving on travel – won't do the job. Even deep cuts along the way generally won't do. You need to think in a different way – to eliminate big chunks of structured cost, to design cost out of the product and system, and to greatly improve efficiencies everywhere.

Understanding Costs and Profits

An important reason companies get their costs out of phase with their competitors' is that they don't usually know what their true costs are. To ascertain costs, you must be able to answer accurately the following questions for each important product, market, or account:

1. What are the directly attributable and fully allocated costs for each major product line, from procurement to customer delivery, including postsale service and warranties?

2. What is the present break-even point, how does it relate to capacity, and how much can volume be increased before it will have to move up?

3. What is the incremental cost and profit on each unit that is produced and sold over the current break-even point?

4. How do costs change with changes in volume? What costs are inescapable if volume declines?

5. How do the current cost structure, capacity utilization, and historical cost trends compare with those of competitors? What cost advantages or disadvantages exist?

Most managers, and particularly those in multi-product-line businesses, routinely make critical decisions without these facts. Managers in rapidly growing businesses are especially uninformed. Both are vulnerable to serious troubles.

Consider a manufacturer of plastic injection-molding machines with a 20-year record of successful growth and profits. The company generated reasonable profits during down cycles by reducing the work force and bringing back into its plant a lot of work that had been subcontracted out in good times. To improve margins, management invested heavily in automated equipment and decided to reduce subcontracting greatly. Projected returns were very attractive. But in the next downturn in capital spending, losses accumulated for the first time in 20 years. The investment in automated equipment had raised the fixed costs and the break-even point significantly. The latitude to reduce costs by eliminating direct labor hours and subcontract work no longer existed. No one had raised this point when the company had evaluated the new equipment.

Revisiting Accounting 101

Most managers agree that it is important to understand the costs and profits of their businesses, though often they don't know what that really means. Those who do know are often frustrated because their information systems do not present the data to develop this understanding, and they don't know what to do about it.

To resolve this problem, let's go back to basic accounting principles. In the table "Common Cost/ Profit Ranges," we have added target ranges for the key cost/profit components of one kind of manufacturing operation and created a framework for developing an initial understanding of cost/profit structures and requirements. The ranges would be quite different for a process industry because of the much higher plant and equipment investment with the consequent greater pressure for high-capacity utilization. The opposite is true of most service businesses with lower investments and fixed costs.

Common Cost/Profit Ranges

Sales		100%
Cost of Goods		65% and down
Gross Margin		35% and up
R&D	0%–15%	
Sales	5%–15%	
General and Administrative	10%–15%	
Total	15%–45%	
Earnings-Before-Taxes Target		15%
Assets Employed		60%
ROA Target (after tax)		15% and up

The framework in the table is designed to yield a sustainable 15% to 20% pretax profit on sales, a 30% to 40% pretax return on assets employed, and a somewhat higher return on equity, depending on the amount of debt leverage in the capital structure. These profit returns must be achieved in order to be a truly outstanding profit performer. Operating consistently within this framework requires the following:

1. Manufacturing operations must generate a gross margin (after all manufacturing costs, including variances) of at least 35% to 40% (and in many cases, much higher) to cover research and development and market-development costs.

2. R&D activities for product and process technology obviously vary by industry but can range up to as high as 15% of sales, depending on the nature of the business and the stage in the product's life cycle.

3. Sales expense typically runs in the 5% to 10% range – lower if sales agents or distributors are used, higher in the early stages of market development.

4. General and administrative cost is usually in the 10% to 15% range and should include all the overhead costs of conducting the business, including interest (at least for working capital) and allocated division, group, or corporate overhead.

5. Total assets employed for plant and equipment and working capital should not run more than about 60 cents on each dollar of sales in a manufacturing company, with variations in the split between them, depending on the type of business.

A company can be profitable if its performance does not fall precisely into this framework. In fact, the ranges show that there will probably be significant differences in the percentage for any cost element, depending on the nature of the industry and its business strategy. *Two numbers are crucial*, however, to meet or exceed the profit targets shown. First is the gross margin, which is the profit-generating fuel for any business. *No manufacturing business can con-*

tinuously generate satisfactory profits if gross margins drop much below 40%. Even this margin rate is questionable unless it is clear that R&D and sales, general, and administrative (SG&A) requirements are near the low end of the ranges shown. There simply aren't enough margin dollars to cover the costs of doing business and still generate a 15% to 20% pretax profit. The business may be able to generate attractive profit margins if it can operate with less R&D and/or SG&A expense. Given the pace of technology, however, most manufacturing businesses cannot sustain product and market position while effectively managing and controlling the business with less cost in expense areas. Pursuing a "copier" or "follower" strategy means R&D expense is probably on the low end of the range, but that doesn't mean that it is zero or that SG&A is necessarily less.

The 60% of sales allowed for total assets employed is also a key number. While this percentage again will vary widely, depending on the nature of the business, it is a reasonably good standard for most manufacturing companies. It is clear that the busi-

> **Too many managers try to improve profits by building volume while ignoring their cost/profit structure.**

ness must generate higher earnings than indicated in our framework in order to yield the desired return if the percentage of total assets to sales is higher. Conversely, the earnings could be much lower and still yield a satisfactory return if the assets were lower, as they are, for example, in many distributor or service businesses.

None of this should come as a surprise to anyone who has been involved in the business world. But it is surprising to find so many managers who continue to struggle to improve profit results by building volume without focusing on basic problems in their cost/profit structure. The problems become readily apparent in this framework. While it is always nice to have more volume, the bottom line will not be helped much if the cost/profit structure is out of line.

The inescapable fact is that any industrial or high-tech company must have a cost/profit structure that makes sense in order to be an attractive profit contributor over the long term. It is essential to first determine what it should be for each particular business and then to make sure the business actually operates around this structure. For no amount of hard work or management brilliance will lead to outstanding profit returns if the business's basic cost/ profit structure is not sound.

The Cycle of Decay

When profits decline or disappear, companies might tighten the belt in the wrong way in the wrong places. This can easily generate a self-feeding cycle of competitive decay. There is a natural tendency for managers to shortchange sales or market development, R&D, or forgo manufacturing improvements for the short term to make the business and profits look better.

The diagram "The Self-Feeding Cycle of Competitive Decay" shows how a viciously deteriorating cycle can work itself out into worsening conditions. The most common (and almost most hidden) thing that sets off such a cycle is management operating with the wrong type of data—that of accounting rather than that of control. Unfortunately, most data management uses are derived from accounting systems designed primarily to meet outside financial reporting requirements.

In addition, these data present aggregate numbers for "large chunks" of business rather than costs or profits for a number of discrete product/market businesses. Even when the data present the cost and profit picture for individual product lines, they are often focused on gross or operating margins, not the true picture after all manufacturing, engineering, sales, and administrative overhead costs are taken into account. Finally, traditional accounting systems typically do not provide a clear picture of how costs and profits behave as unit volume moves up or down. Thus they are not particularly helpful to managers who must evaluate sales, marketing, and manufacturing alternatives that involve different levels of activity.

For these reasons, you should reorganize, reorder, and reformulate these financial data. This may mean extra effort, but it is not as difficult as it sounds. First, you must agree on a few commonsense cost definitions that provide the basis for categorizing all costs associated with each

product or product-line business. The following cost categories can provide a definitive framework for any manager.

1. *Bedrock Fixed.* These costs are related to physical capacity and include plant and equipment costs such as depreciation, taxes, and facility maintenance that cannot be avoided unless the facility is sold or written off the books. These are the only true fixed costs. Typically, they are not as large a factor in the cost strucure of companies as you would think, though they become greater as companies automate.

2. *Managed Fixed.* These costs are largely related to people and structure—the so-called "overhead" of management, accounting, finance—and even activities like advertising, sales, R&D, or market development. All tend to build up as a business grows. Once in place, managers often treat them as integral and bedrock fixed costs. They are not. You can and should manage them. Understanding their makeup is important to keeping them under control and distinguishing them from the overhead costs that organizations share.

3. *Direct Variable Costs.* These costs rise or fall directly in proportion to the business volume. They are easily identified and can be traced back to the specific units produced or services rendered where, again, they can be better examined and managed.

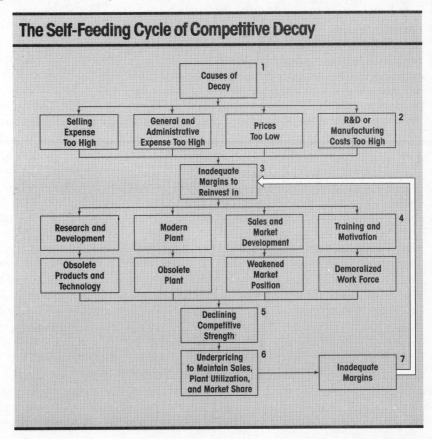

The Self-Feeding Cycle of Competitive Decay

Most Costs Are Manageable – Few Are Fixed or Variable

Bedrock Fixed	Managed				Truly Variable
Depreciation	Property Tax	Supervision	Small Tools	Telephone	Materials
Patent Amortization	Rent	Inspection	Lighting	Receiving	Royalties
	Cleaning	Payroll Taxes	Materials Services	Spoilage	Overtime Premium
	Maintenance of Building	Payroll Services	Machinery Maintenance	Benefits	Supplies
	Insurance	Office Expenses	Lubricants	Wages	Fuel
	Executive Salaries	Advertising	Sales Salaries		Power
	Auditing Expense	Administrative Salaries	Entertainment		Scrap
		Legal Expense	Travel		Commissions
			Uncollectible Accounts		Freight

4. *Shared Costs.* These are all the other costs incurred to support the business that are not readily traceable to any one product or line or activity. They normally include overhead of the corporation, division, and/or plant, as well as selling and general and administrative expenses. They can also include operating costs for plant and equipment. All are manageable.

Agreeing on these cost definitions is the first step. The second step is assigning the various operating costs to these classifications. In most businesses, few costs are either absolutely fixed or variable. Most costs lie in the vast area of managed costs shown in the accompanying table "Most Costs Are Manageable."

Make no mistake, costs in the managed category are not fixed, even though they are commonly bundled under this label. Generally, as a business expands, costs tend to be far more variable than they should be, and when it contracts, they are far more fixed than they should be.

Once there is agreement on these cost categories and definitions, the next step is getting help from the accounting or controller's department to determine how to divide and assign to specific product/market businesses the costs incurred in each of these categories. This is not easily done. Many accountants are reluctant to divide fixed costs into these categories or to allocate shared costs to specific product areas, because it is impossible to do this with the precision that accounting professionals normally use to develop traditional financial statements. There is a natural aversion to shifting numbers around in any imprecise manner. There is simply no way, however, to know how well or how badly a product or product line is doing without getting these cost data clear— without knowing which are bedrock fixed, managed fixed, direct variable, or shared and without allocat-

ing them to their various business units and product lines. At the divisional or business unit level, cross-functional teams of all the department heads and the general manager should be responsible for hammering out the allocations according to the actual activity levels of each cost category.

In many cases, general management must ensure that the data are reordered along the lines necessary for intelligent product/market management. Shared costs are a particularly difficult problem for most companies and difficult to attack as a lump. You must break them down and assign them to discrete business units or product lines, even if it means being "arbitrary" by some standard. Managers with hands-on profit responsibility will argue about the fairness of the allocations. But it is critical to take a stand lest discussions get endless, acrimonious, and fruitless. There is no other way. Allocating all costs is the only way to know what is really going on.

The table "Full Costing Changes the Profit Picture" shows the result of changing to full-cost allocations in the instrumentation division of a large corporation. When done, product groups traditionally regarded as the best profit producers were not as profitable as everyone thought, and some of the worst were actually near the best.

The instrumentation division overall had a reported gross margin of 45.6% and a generated 11% pretax profit of $30.1 million. Sales and gross margins were reported by product line, but pretax profit was reported only for the division overall. Reported gross margins for the product groups varied from a high of 54% to a low of 40%. Fully loading all producing lines with their real costs resulted in adjusted gross margins that varied between 38.1% and 15.9%. Because of their relatively lower reported gross margins, standard products D and E (at 41% and 40% respectively) had often taken a backseat when the

Full Costing Changes the Profit Picture *(in millions of dollars)*

Product Group	Annual Sales	Reported Gross Margin		Reported Pretax Profit		Adjusted Gross Margin		Adjusted Pretax Profit	
A	$ 42	$ 22.7	54%	NA	NA	$ 19.8	47.0%	$ 3.7	8.8%
B	51	26.5	52	NA	NA	23.4	46.8	4.0	7.8
C	37	17.4	47	NA	NA	15.9	43.0	3.4	9.2
D	83	34.0	41	NA	NA	38.1	46.0	12.1	14.6
E	61	24.4	40	NA	NA	27.8	45.6	6.9	11.3
Division-wide	$274	$125.0	45.6%	$30.1	11.0%	$125.0	45.6%	$30.1	11.0%

company assigned sales, manufacturing, and engineering priorities. When it analyzed and allocated plant, engineering, and SG&A overheads according to actual need or usage, it was clear that the standard products were being penalized by standard formulas that distributed these overheads according to sales volume. Adjusted gross margin percentages for standard products D and E improved their relative pretax profit performance dramatically; gross margins on custom-engineered products A, B, and C declined by several percentage points once appropriate overhead costs were allocated against them.

Looked at in another way, products D and E contributed less than half (48.6%) of reported gross-

> **Get commitment to cost management by sharing your known cost-profit facts with many in the business unit.**

margin dollars but almost two-thirds (63.1%) of pretax-profit dollars after all costs were allocated. It is obvious that the way that management assigns its sales, manufacturing, and engineering priorities can change drastically once the actual cost-profit pictures become clear.

Net profitability statements also help bring management pressure on big chunks of overhead or shared costs (for example, SG&A, engineering, manufacturing, and corporate overheads) that are otherwise difficult to evaluate and control. When companies allocate these costs to specific products or profit centers, they show up as a charge against earnings, and managers responsible for profits carefully scrutinize and challenge them. This can be a powerful force toward reducing and getting large chunks of

overhead costs under control that would otherwise never be scrutinized by someone with a direct profit responsibility.

Strategic and Daily Considerations

Selecting Product/Market Segments. Knowing the true cost and profit structure for product groups is also an immense help in selecting products, markets, and customers for emphasis. Remarkably few managers consider profit potentials when they assess and select product/market segments. They more often focus on sales potential—with the assumption that profits will follow. Managers can justify this in a company's or a product's early stages but never later. When the fight for share in a stable or slow-growth or declining market intensifies, managers must specialize in what's more profitable rather than in what's bigger.

Companywide Cost-Profit Awareness. Once costs are known and detailed for product lines, markets, and key customers, you should share detailed cost and profit information with many people in the business unit. If top and general management confine the known cost-profit facts to a select few who "need to know" them, fewer people will feel committed to cost management.

William LaMothe, chairman and CEO of Kellogg, the $4 billion ready-to-eat-cereal manufacturer, said in an interview, "At Kellogg's, we all focus on details, and cost details are a big part of that. By being geared to saving pennies on everything we do, that turns into a lot of dollars when you're dealing with the volumes we move. Hand-in-hand with driving unit costs down is the need for leading-edge production technology and an obsession about quality. As a result, we can produce a box of cereal at a lower unit cost than anyone else in the world. We have many teams of production workers that are responsible for keeping quality up and keeping costs down....We have a very disciplined approach to costs across and up and down the organization. We spend a lot of time talking about costs, because cereal is the only business we have. The drumbeat is that we will remain a lower cost supplier. Kellogg's has earned a ten-year average EPS growth of 12.5% and a ten-year average return on capital of 26% and our return on equity for the same period is approximately 40%."

Managing Cash and Liquidity. Finally, there is the matter of cash. Cash returns can be more important than reported profits. Cash returns lead to liquidity, and liquidity is a top priority whenever there are high risks and great uncertainties. Cash and liquidity help withstand surprises, facilitate adaptation to sudden changes, and can help you capitalize on the narrower windows of opportunity that are common in a turbulent environment.

Any entrepreneur who has lived through a startup and built a market position knows the importance of cash and liquidity. A business can go bankrupt while reporting profits. But it will never go bankrupt as long as its cash and liquidity positions are strong. Most senior corporate executives understand this, but many do not make sure it is sufficiently stressed or understood at the operating level.

The results are apparent in most corporations. Capital expenditure proposals tend to be "wish lists" justified on projected volume gains or cost savings without regard to the availability of funds or to cash-carrying costs. Working capital is allowed to build without adequate regard for its carrying costs. Over-investment in plant, equipment, and working capital often disguises sloppy business practices and control. These are practices that inevitably lead to a bloated investment base—too big for the business and too marginal for profits.

Many operating managers are unaware of the costs of excessive capital tie-ups. For example, most of them will acknowledge that it costs money to carry their inventory—these days, usually 8% or 9%. But few know that total carrying costs should include storage, taxes, obsolescence, and shrinkage, and that total costs (including interest) actually run closer to 30%. The reason that so few managers know this is that the costs of working capital are not charged against their earnings, even though they are real costs of doing business.

A manager who makes pricing, capital investment, personnel, and even strategic and/or tactical decisions without this product/market cost infor-

> ## Reward systems should pay only those who meet cash objectives—and penalize those who don't.

mation—and then does not create a companywide discipline to manage costs—will face unpleasant surprises and serious questions of survival as the competitive world gets increasingly turbulent.

Cash management deserves far greater attention than it gets in most companies. Management must put more emphasis on, and be held accountable for, managing liquidity. Planning and reporting systems should be modified to highlight actual cash flow and liquidity against objectives. Finally, the reward system should be adjusted to pay those who meet cash objectives and penalize those who don't.

None of these actions are difficult if senior management has the will and as long as the accounting system is set up to do so. They can be impossible, however, if the accounting systems are designed around big divisions of business rather than around discrete product/market segments and if big chunks of structured or managed fixed costs are not divided and allocated to these smaller business units.

Ideally, every manager should think like a small-business entrepreneur whose own money is at risk and who has little of it at hand. If managers did this, we would see fewer companies with bloated balance sheets and marginal returns and see lots more that thrive efficiently.

Reprint 90102

Getting Things Done

Why SG&A doesn't always work

Thomas S. Dudick

With global competition increasing, U.S. manufacturing companies are giving their nonmanufacturing costs much closer scrutiny than they've traditionally done and with good reason. Over the past ten years, selling, general, and administrative (SG&A) expenses have been rising as a percentage of the total cost of doing business. Today, because of higher selling, advertising, warehousing, and other costs, it's not unusual for SG&A to approach 50% or more of a company's manufacturing costs. In the high-technology sector, SG&A can easily approach 100% of manufacturing expenses.

To achieve better control over nonmanufacturing costs, manufacturing executives are developing more precise measures of their SG&A expenses. Many manufacturing companies, however, continue to make the mistake of relying on "one size fits all" methods of allocating SG&A costs. I have observed this process many times in the course of my work as a manufacturing cost consultant. It can be found in every industry and in companies that are well managed in other respects.

In organizations that take a production-line approach to SG&A, the controller typically uses the percent-of-sales, cost-of-sales, or some other arbitrary method of allocation. When percent of sales, one of the most common methods, is used, the corporate controller simply divides the total corporate sales revenue into the total companywide SG&A expense and applies

the resulting percentage to all product lines. If, for example, the company's SG&A cost is 10% of its sales revenue, then that's the percentage the company controller will charge to each product line based on its sales. Under the cost-of-sales method, the controller charges each product line an SG&A amount based on its share of manufacturing cost (materials, direct labor, and factory overhead).

> *"Broadbrush SG&A accounting methods can distort the profitability of a company's different product lines and market segments."*

Although the use of such standardized, across-the-board methods simplifies SG&A cost accounting for company accountants working under the pressure of having to meet financial reporting deadlines, these arbitrary measures can distort the profitability of a company's different product lines and market segments. Profits can be inflated and losses understated using broadbrush SG&A accounting methods. While a variety of distortions

are possible, there are, as we shall see, several ways of correcting for them.

Materials cost distortions

When a company's raw materials costs vary greatly among its product lines, severe distortions in SG&A costs can result if accountants use conventional percent-of-sales or cost-of-sales methods of allocation.

The president of a sewing notions company I know of had been puzzled by the profit performance of his woolen goods line. Although his woolen goods sales had been steadily increasing, the line showed a loss. Because wool had a higher materials cost than the company's other products, it had a low gross margin. The president discovered that the profit for the woolen goods line was being penalized because the company's use of the percent-of-sales expensing formula meant that wool's high materials cost resulted in an overstatement of its SG&A costs.

The company controller suggested that they use a conversion cost ratio, which would eliminate profit distortions caused by differences in raw materials costs. To construct the conversion ratio, the controller added up the company's direct factory labor and overhead and divided it into the total SG&A expense. He used the resulting conversion ratio to allocate SG&A costs to each product line based on each line's direct factory labor and overhead. Now the woolen goods line showed a profit, while the other lines showed reduced net income.

Although a conversion cost ratio is usually an improvement over the percent-of-sales method, it too has built-in distortions and therefore should be used with caution. If a company has

Mr. Dudick does consulting work for the accounting firm of Ernst & Whinney in cost systems, product costing, pricing, and manufacturing cost and operating controls. He has served as budget director for Allen B. DuMont Laboratories, plant controller for GTE Sylvania, and internal consultant for the Raytheon Company. He is the author of Dudick on Manufacturing Cost Controls *(Prentice-Hall, 1985), among other books.*

certain product lines with a high percentage of finished components bought from vendors, those lines will incur much lower conversion costs. Their SG&A charges would be understated and their profitability inflated.

Fine-tuning SG&A costs

Is there a better method? Since any across-the-board measure – including a conversion ratio – can lead to distorted perceptions of profitability, the best solution is to develop a finely tuned allocation method that will give more precise measures of the SG&A costs incurred by each of a company's product lines. Each of the following cases illustrates how a specific type of distortion can be avoided using more accurate SG&A cost information.

Product-line distortions

Confronted with intensifying foreign and domestic competition, the senior management of an electronics company decided to review its manufacturing and nonmanufacturing costs. As part of that review, it looked at how the company's accountants were calculating SG&A expenses for each of the corporation's major product lines.

Up to that time, the company's accounting staff had been using the percent-of-sales method for allocating SG&A expenses to each of the manufacturing divisions. Some division managers were dissatisfied with the result, among them the vice president of the television division. He complained that his division's SG&A charge was inflated because his product line used high-cost finished components – picture tubes and cabinets.

The problem arose because these components had a high percentage of materials content in the selling price. This inflated his division's SG&A allocation in comparison with other divisions whose materials content was much lower as a percentage of sales. As Part A of *Exhibit I* shows, the television line had a pretax loss of 3.9% using the percent-of-sales method. Its share of total corporate SG&A was 24% during that period. To get a more accurate measure of each line's profit-and-loss performance, a specialist from marketing

and another from manufacturing services developed a more precise SG&A allocation formula.

The marketing specialist pointed out that reliable information was readily available to break down the selling expenses for each product line. Fully 90% of the selling cost consisted of payroll expenses. After the specialist identified which product lines were handled by the different salespeople, the annual payroll costs for each product line could be calculated. The remaining nonpayroll component, 10% of the cost, was allocated on the same basis as the other 90%. Warehousing costs could be allocated to each product line by counting the number of bays used to store each product. Percentage rates of space utilization could then be calculated by product line.

Advertising expenses would continue to be allocated on the traditional percent-of-sales basis because the company's advertising campaigns usually promoted the corporation and its entire product line as a whole. Allocating promotional costs posed no problem either because promotions were always carried out on an individual product-line basis.

The manufacturing services specialist recommended that the corporate purchasing department charge each product line according to the amount of material it actually used. Formerly, corporate purchasing had consolidated the purchase of high-volume materials used in all product lines. He recommended that the industrial relations department charge each product line according to its percentage share of the total number of employees. Finally, he suggested that corporate accounting and data processing costs be parceled out to the various product lines on the following basis:

Payroll costs would be charged based on the number of employees in each division.

Customer billing costs would be allocated according to the number of invoices or invoice lines for each division.

Sales reports prepared by corporate staff would be allocated on the basis of the same ratio used to charge sales office overhead to each product line.

Internal auditing expenses would be charged to each product line

by multiplying the number of auditor days spent in each division by the auditor's per diem fee.

The manufacturing services specialist also suggested that corporate quality control costs be divided according to the number of QC employees assigned to each division. Other corporate services that couldn't easily be charged to each product line could be allocated by simply dividing those costs by the number of product lines. Each line would absorb an equal amount of the costs on the assumption that these services were equally available to all divisions at any time.

Top management implemented the specialists' recommendations. The impact of the new method on the profit performance of each of the company's product lines can be seen in Part B of *Exhibit I*.

The results confirmed what the vice president in charge of the television division had long suspected: his division's financial performance had been depressed under the old SG&A allocation measure. The product-specific SG&A method reduced his division's share of corporate SG&A from 24% to 17.2% and his division's pretax loss from 3.9% to 1.4%. The new method also led to a near doubling of the cathode-ray tube division's profit – from 5.4% to 9.1%.

Market segment distortions

A company's cost accounting system may also fail to capture accurately the SG&A costs of selling to different market segments. A manufacturer of power cords, switches, sockets, and other electrical fixtures sold to three different market segments: original equipment manufacturers, retail outlets (replacement market), and building contractors (distributor market). In the past, the company had made no effort to analyze its SG&A costs by market segment; it simply assessed a flat SG&A percentage against all sales. The company's controller finally recognized the need to allocate SG&A costs based on the real costs of selling to each market. More finely tuned SG&A cost information would give top management a better picture of the true profitability of the different market segments.

The controller requested managers in the different departments

Exhibit I How SG&A cost-allocation methods affect pretax profits

Product line	Part A Conventional percent-of-sales method		Part B New product-specific method	
	SG&A charge as a percentage of total corporate SG&A	Pretax profit	SG&A charge as a percentage of total corporate SG&A	Pretax profit
Television	24.0 %	(3.9) %	17.2 %	(1.4) %
Cathode-ray tubes	17.7	5.4	10.2	9.1
Phosphors	2.0	16.5	1.2	20.0
Television components	27.9	15.4	28.4	15.3
Electronics	2.4	7.4	3.3	4.5
Fabricated parts	6.0	13.1	2.6	17.9
Lighting products	20.0	22.0	37.1	14.5
Total	100.0 %		100.0 %	

Exhibit II Itemized SG&A costs by market segment

Itemized expenses	OEM market	Replacement market	Distributor market
Selling	3.1 %	4.3 %	4.4 %
Warehousing	1.4	2.7	2.4
Packing	1.7	3.5	2.5
Advertising and promotion	1.8	3.5	3.2
Bad debts	0.1	0.9	0.3
Freight	0.9	2.0	1.3
Administration*	2.6	2.3	2.6
Total SG&A as a percentage of sales	11.6 %	19.2 %	16.7 %

*Administration includes any remaining costs after direct charges have been made to the various manufacturing units. The direct charges include such services as payroll, billing, accounts payable, and any other corporate charges that can be specifically identified by location. These represent costs that would have been incurred by the individual plants as manufacturing overhead if they were completely decentralized.

to calculate advertising, warehousing, selling, and other nonmanufacturing costs for the three market segments. Warehousing costs, for example, could be parceled out according to the space used in serving the different market groups. The hours spent by the sales force in the field were also logged and allocated to the different market segments.

As *Exhibit II* shows, the new method for allocating SG&A revealed substantial disparities in costs among the three segments in most expense categories—disparities not caused by differences in the kinds of electrical products sold in each market.

Freight, packing, and warehousing costs, for example, were much lower for the OEM market than for the other two markets. The reason, the controller learned, was that OEMs typically order in bulk. Packing and freight costs for the replacement market were much higher because orders placed by hardware stores and other retailers are usually smaller and more varied. The cost of selling to the OEM market was also lower because the company's salespeople didn't have to call on OEM accounts as frequently as on accounts in the other two markets. What top management learned was that the OEM market was more profitable than had been assumed.

Distortions caused by low volume

The percent-of-sales method for allocating SG&A costs can be especially troublesome when sales of one product line constitute a very small percentage of total sales. The CEO of a sunglasses manufacturing company decided to add a line of hair combs. Because demand for sunglasses is seasonal, he had excess capacity on his plastic-molding machines. He would incur no additional selling costs because his salespeople could easily sell the comb line when calling on their sunglasses accounts.

The CEO told the controller to charge the comb line for its fair share of SG&A costs, and the controller did so using the percent-of-sales method. The marketing group had projected that combs would account for 15% of the company's $21.5 million in total revenue, and the controller used that percentage to calculate the comb line's share of SG&A. (The comb line's share of revenue was small because its unit cost was much lower than that of the sunglasses line.)

The company's SG&A expense (excluding sales commissions) was assessed as a fixed monthly cost. Based on sales projections, total SG&A would amount to approximately $3.8 million a year (or 18% of total sales). The controller apportioned 15% of the monthly SG&A charge ($48,462) to combs and 85% ($274,620) to sunglasses.

The comb line's low share of total revenues led to erratic fluctuations in its profit performance. When sunglasses sales dipped during the off-season, the effect on the comb line's share of sales was magnified—because of the comb line's smaller percentage of revenue. The SG&A cost for sunglasses varied no more than three percentage points, from 11% in April to 14% in June. In sharp contrast, the SG&A cost for combs swung from 21% in April to 13% in June.

As the controller explained to the CEO, the erratic profit performance of the comb line resulted from the magnified impact of the sharp change in sunglasses sales on the comb line's percentage of revenue. This caused combs to be overcharged for SG&A. More sales effort was required to sell sunglasses; advertising, promotion, and packaging costs were also much higher for sunglasses.

The controller solved the problem by charging the comb line a flat 5% of total corporate SG&A. This reduced the variability in the comb line's SG&A from 7% of sales in April to 4% of sales in June. He explained that although month-to-month variation in profitability would still occur, the profit figures for combs would be more accurate and stable using the new, more realistic SG&A percentage figure.

When companies rely on undifferentiated, "one size fits all" cost accounting methods without regard to important differences among product lines and markets, measures of profitability can become distorted. Since SG&A costs can vary widely among a company's products or markets, more precise methods for allocating SG&A will give management a more accurate reading of each product line's profit.

There is, however, an important caveat to be made. Corporate controllers must decide how far to go in breaking down SG&A expenses. It may not pay, for example, to count the number of phone calls made or salesperson hours spent in the field per account in allocating selling costs to a product line. Too much refinement may impose unjustifiable record-keeping costs.

A good case can be made, however, that reasonably detailed breakdowns should be carried out since in most cases SG&A percentage breakdowns will need to be made only once during the year, when the annual financial plan is developed. With more accurate cost and profit measures, management can know which product lines and markets most deserve corporate resources and attention. ▽

Reprint 87106

SPECIAL REPORT

How control systems support manufacturing excellence

Another Hidden Edge – Japanese Management Accounting

by TOSHIRO HIROMOTO

Much has been written about why Japanese manufacturers continue to outperform their U.S. competitors in cost, quality, and on-time delivery. Most experts point to practices like just-in-time production, total quality control, and the aggressive use of flexible manufacturing technologies. One area that has received less attention, but that I believe contributes mightily to Japanese competitiveness, is how many companies' management accounting systems reinforce a top-to-bottom commitment to process and product innovation.

I have studied management accounting systems at Japanese companies in several major industries including automobiles, computers, consumer electronics, and semiconductors. Although practices varied greatly, several related patterns did emerge. These patterns differentiate certain aspects of Japanese management accounting from established practices in the United States.

Like their U.S. counterparts, Japanese companies must value inventory for tax purposes and financial statements. But the Japanese don't let these accounting procedures determine how they measure and control organizational activities. Japanese companies tend to use their management control systems to support and reinforce their manufacturing strategies. A more direct link therefore exists between management accounting practices and corporate goals.

Japanese companies seem to use accounting systems more to motivate employees to act in accordance with long-term manufacturing strategies than to provide senior management with precise data on costs, variances, and profits. Accounting plays more of an "influencing" role than an "informing" role. For example, high-level Japanese managers seem to worry less about whether an overhead allocation system reflects the precise demands each product

makes on corporate resources than about how the system affects the cost-reduction priorities of middle managers and shop-floor workers. As a result, they sometimes use allocation techniques that executives in the United States might dismiss as simplistic or even misguided.

Accounting in Japan also reflects and reinforces an overriding commitment to market-driven management. When estimating costs on new products, for example, many companies make it a point not to rely completely on prevailing engineering standards. Instead, they establish target costs derived from estimates of a competitive market price. These target costs are usually well below currently achievable costs, which are based on standard technologies and processes. Managers then set benchmarks to measure incremental progress toward meeting the target cost objectives.

Several companies I studied also de-emphasize standard cost systems for monitoring factory performance. In general, Japanese management accounting does not stress optimizing within existing constraints. Rather, it encourages employees to make continual improvements by tightening those constraints.

The following cases highlight some of the differences between management accounting in Japan and the United States. My intention is to be suggestive, not definitive. Not all Japanese companies use the techniques I describe, and some U.S. companies have adopted approaches similar to what I have seen in Japan.

Allocating overhead

American executives have been barraged with criticism about how long-accepted techniques for allocating manufacturing overhead can distort product costs and paint a flawed

Toshiro Hiromoto is an associate professor of accounting at Hitotsubashi University in Tokyo. He recently spent two years in the United States as a visiting scholar at Stanford University and the Harvard Business School. He has written extensively on accounting and management in Japan.

picture of the profitability of manufacturing operations. Accounting experts challenge direct labor hours as an overhead allocation base since direct labor represents only a small percentage of total costs in most manufacturing environments. They argue that a logical and causal relationship should exist between the overhead burden and the assignment of costs to individual products. They believe that an allocation system should capture as precisely as possible the reality of shop-floor costs.

Japanese companies are certainly aware of this perspective, but many of the companies I examined don't seem to share it. Consider the practices of the Hitachi division that operates the world's largest factory devoted exclusively to videocassette recorders. The Hitachi VCR plant is highly automated yet continues to use direct labor as the basis for allocating manufacturing overhead. Overhead allocation doesn't reflect the actual production process in the factory's automated environment. When I asked the accountants whether that policy might lead to bad decisions, they responded with an emphatic no. Hitachi, like many large Japanese manufacturers, is convinced that reducing direct labor is essential for ongoing cost improvement. The company is committed to aggressive automation to promote long-term competitiveness. Allocating overhead based on direct labor creates the desired strong pro-automation incentives throughout the organization.

The perspective offered by Hitachi managers seems to be shared by their counterparts at many other companies. It is more important, they argue, to have an overhead allocation system (and other aspects of management accounting) that motivates employees to work in harmony with the company's long-term goals than to pinpoint production costs. Japanese managers want their accounting systems to help create a competitive future, not quantify the performance of their organizations at this moment.

Another Hitachi factory (this one in the refrigeration and air-conditioning equipment sector) employs an overhead allocation technique, based on the number of parts in product models, to influence its engineers' design decisions. Japanese companies have long known what more and more U.S. companies are now recognizing—that the number of parts in a product, especially custom parts, directly relates to the amount of overhead. Manufacturing costs increase with the complexity of the production process, as measured, for example, by the range of products built in a factory or the number of parts per product. In plants assembling diverse products, reducing the number of parts and promoting the use of standard parts across product lines can lower costs dramatically.

Using standard parts can also lower materials costs, insofar as it creates possibilities for more aggressive volume buying. Yet on a product-by-product basis, many cost systems fail to recognize these economies.

Consider a factory building several different products. The products all use one or both of two

> # The secret of Japanese management accounting: integrate it into corporate strategy.

parts, A and B, which the factory buys in roughly equal amounts. Most of the products use both parts. The unit cost of part A is $7, of part B, $10. Part B has more capabilities than part A; in fact, B can replace A. If the factory doubles its purchases of part B, it qualifies for a discounted $8 unit price. For products that incorporate both parts, substituting B for A makes sense to qualify for the discount. (The total parts cost is $17 using A and B, $16 using Bs only.) Part B, in other words, should become a standard part for the factory. But departments building products that use only part A may be reluctant to accept the substitute part B because even discounted, the cost of B exceeds that of A.

This factory needs an accounting system that motivates departments to look beyond their parochial interests for the sake of enterprise-level cost reduction. Hitachi has adopted such an approach by adding overhead surcharges to products that use nonstandard parts. The more custom parts in a product, the higher the overhead charge.

Accounting for market-driven design

By the time a new product enters the manufacturing stage, opportunities to economize significantly are limited. As the Hitachi refrigerator example suggests, Japanese companies have long recognized that the design stage holds the greatest promise for supporting low-cost production. Many U.S. manufacturers, including Texas Instruments, Hewlett-Packard, and Ford, are also making competitive strides in this area. But certain Japanese companies have taken the process even further. They don't simply design products to make better use of technologies and work flows; they design and build products that will meet the price required for market success—whether or not that price is supported by current manufacturing practices. Their management accounting systems incorporate this commitment.

Daihatsu Motor Company, a medium-sized automobile producer that has yet to enter the U.S. market, provides a good example of market-driven accounting practices. It installed the *genka kikaku* product development system in its factories soon after affiliating with Toyota, which pioneered the approach. The *genka kikaku* process at Daihatsu usually lasts three years, at which time the new car goes into production. The process begins when the *shusa* (the product manager responsible for a new car from planning through sales) instructs the functional departments to submit the features and performance specifications that they believe the car should include. The *shusa* then makes

"Sure, real estate prices are sky-high, but kings don't sell their castles, and that's that."

recommendations to the senior managers, who issue a development order.

Next comes cost estimation. Management does not simply turn over the development order to the accountants and ask what it would cost to build the car based on existing engineering standards. Rather, Daihatsu establishes a target selling price based on what it believes the market will accept and specifies a target profit margin that reflects the company's strategic plans and financial projections. The difference between these two figures represents the "allowable cost" per car.

In practice, this target cost is far below what realistically can be attained. So each department calculates an "accumulated cost" based on current technologies and practices—that is, the standard cost achievable with no innovation. Finally, management establishes a target cost that represents a middle ground between these two estimates. This adjusted price-profit margin cost becomes the goal toward which everyone works.

At the design stage, engineers working on different parts of the car interact frequently with the various players (purchasing, shop-floor supervisors, parts suppliers) who will implement the final design. As the design process unfolds, the participants compare estimated costs with the target. The variances are fed back to the product developers, and the cycle repeats: design proposals, cost estimates, variance calculations, value engineering analysis to include desired features at the lowest possible cost, and redesign. The cycle ends with the approval of a final design that meets the target cost.

A similar dynamic operates at the production stage, where Daihatsu uses complementary approaches to manage costs: total plant cost management and *dai-atari kanri*, or per-unit cost management.

Reports based on total plant cost management are prepared for senior executives and plant managers. The studies compare budgeted costs with actual costs for an entire factory. Reports generated by the *dai-atari kanri* system are intended for managers at specific workstations. Comparisons between budgeted and actual costs are made only for "variable" charges, which include some costs, like tools, that do not vary strictly with short-term output. Put simply, items subject to *dai-atari kanri* include all costs that can be reduced through workers' continual efforts and process improvement activities—that is, controllable costs.

In production, as in the design stage, Daihatsu does not take a static approach to cost management. During the first year of production for a new car, the budgeted cost reflects targets set during the *genka kikaku* process. This cost is a starting point, however, not an ultimate goal; over the course of the year, it is tightened monthly by a cost-reduction rate based on short-term profit objectives. In subsequent years, the actual cost of the previous period becomes the starting point for further tightening, thereby creating a cost-reduction dynamic for as long as the model remains in production.

Good-bye to standard costs

The market-driven philosophy at Daihatsu and other Japanese companies helps to explain why standard cost systems are not used as widely in Japan as they are in the United States. Standard costs reflect an engineering mind-set and technology-driven management. The goal is to minimize variances between budgeted and actual costs—to perform as closely as possible to best available practice. Market-driven management, on the other hand, emphasizes doing what it takes to achieve a desired performance level under market conditions. How efficiently a company *should* be able to build a product is less important to the Japanese than how efficiently it *must* be able to build it for maximum marketplace success.

Many Japanese companies that have used standard cost systems seem to be moving beyond them.

> **Japanese companies put much more emphasis on measuring the nonfinancial aspects of factory performance.**

NEC, the diversified electronics giant, designed and installed its standard cost system in the 1950s. The company still uses standard cost reports as a factory management tool and continues to train new employees in the system. But NEC recognizes that it has reached a strategic turning point and it is adjusting its management accounting policies accordingly.

NEC installed its standard cost system when it was supplying a stable product range (mostly telephones and exchangers) at stable prices to a large and stable customer, Nippon Telegraph & Telephone (NTT). Today NEC produces a vast array of products subject to rapid obsolescence and technological change. Its product line poses severe challenges to the standard cost system. The cost standards cannot be revised quickly enough for many products, so variance reports are increasingly open to question. (NEC revises its cost standards every six months, and even then only for a subset of products.) As a result, the company is relying more heavily on departmental budgets than product-by-product variances from standard costs. As with

Daihatsu, targets are based on market demands and planned profit levels, and are tightened over time.

The U.S. subsidiary of a major Japanese electronics company takes this budgeting approach even further. Its production and marketing departments operate as separate profit centers. These departments interact to establish internal transfer prices for products. The transfer price is a negotiated percentage of the market price. Under this method, market prices critically influence departmental performance, since market prices are the basis for determining transfer prices. Both the production and marketing functions are encouraged to respond to market demand and competitive trends rather than focus solely on internal indicators.

The company recently extended this approach to its sales department, which is separate from marketing. Selling costs used to be allocated to individual products under a standard cost approach. Now the sales department operates as a profit center and negotiates commission levels with the marketing department. Through the cost system, these commissions are then assigned to products. Thus the marketing department can make product decisions without accepting selling expenses as given, which increases pressure on the sales force to operate as efficiently as possible.

Accounting and strategy

The accounting practices I have described do not necessarily represent Japanese practices as a whole. They do, however, point to a central principle that seems to guide management accounting in Japan—that accounting policies should be subservient to corporate strategy, not independent of it. Japanese manufacturing strategy places high premiums on quality and timely delivery in addition to low-cost production. Thus companies make extensive use, certainly more than many of their U.S. competitors, of nonfinancial measures to evaluate factory performance. The reason is straightforward: if a management accounting system measures only

costs, employees tend to focus on costs exclusively.

I have encountered many practices designed to capture the nonfinancial dimensions of factory performance. One Japanese automaker wanted to motivate its managers and employees to reduce throughput time in assembly operations. It recognized that direct labor hours measure costs, not the actual time required to build and ship a car. So for time-management purposes, the company has replaced direct labor hours with a variable called managed hours per unit. In addition to direct labor, this new measure incorporates the time required for nonproductive activities like equipment maintenance and product repairs.

In an effort to improve machine and equipment efficiency, many companies are emphasizing preventive and corrective maintenance over breakdown maintenance. (Corrective maintenance means redesigning equipment to reduce failures and facilitate routine maintenance.) This emphasis goes beyond exhorting shop-floor personnel to pay more attention to their machines. Companies regularly measure rates of unexpected equipment failures, ratios of preventive and corrective maintenance to total maintenance, and other variables that track machine performance. These results are widely distributed and evaluated during small group discussions in the factory.

For companies to maintain competitive advantage, employees must be continually innovative. This requires motivation. A product designer must be motivated to play a significant role in cost reduction. Shop-floor workers and supervisors must constantly strive to improve efficiency beyond what "best practice" currently dictates. The Japanese have demonstrated that management accounting can play a significant role in integrating the innovative efforts of employees with the company's long-term strategies and goals.

Reprint 88406

Must CIM be justified by faith alone?

"Managers need not – and should not – abandon the effort to justify computer-integrated manufacturing on financial grounds. Instead, they need ways to apply the DCF approach more appropriately."

Robert S. Kaplan

When the Yamazaki Machinery Company in Japan installed an $18 million flexible manufacturing system, the results were truly startling: a reduction in machines from 68 to 18, in employees from 215 to 12, in the floor space needed for production from 103,000 square feet to 30,000, and in average processing time from 35 days to 1.5.[1] After two years, however, total savings came to only $6.9 million, $3.9 million of which had flowed from a one-time cut in inventory. Even if the system continued to produce annual labor savings of $1.5 million for 20 years, the project's return would be less than 10% per year. Since many U.S. companies use hurdle rates of 15% or higher and payback periods of five years or less, they would find it hard to justify this investment in new technology – despite its enormous savings in number of employees, floor space, inventory, and throughput times.

The apparent inability of traditional modes of financial analysis like discounted cash flow to justify investments in computer-integrated manufacturing (CIM) has led a growing number of managers and observers to propose abandoning such criteria for CIM-related investments. "Let's be more practical," runs one such opinion. "DCF is not the only gospel. Many managers have become too absorbed with DCF to the extent that practical strategic directional considerations have been overlooked."[2]

Faced with outdated and inappropriate procedures of investment analysis, all that responsible executives can do is cast them aside in a bold leap of strategic faith. "Beyond all else," they have come to be-

Mr. Kaplan is Arthur Lowes Dickinson Professor of Accounting at the Harvard Business School and a professor of industrial administration at Carnegie-Mellon University, where for six years he was dean of the business school. His first article for HBR, "Yesterday's Accounting Undermines Production" (July-August 1984), was a McKinsey Award winner.

lieve, "capital investment represents an act of faith, a belief that the future will be as promising as the present, together with a commitment to making the future happen."[3]

But must there be a fundamental conflict between the financial and the strategic justifications for CIM? It is unlikely that the theory of discounting future cash flow is either faulty or unimportant: receiving $1 in the future is worth less than receiving $1 today. If a company, even for good strategic reasons, consistently invests in projects whose financial returns are below its cost of capital, it will be on the road to insolvency. Whatever the special values of CIM technology, they cannot reverse the logic of the time value of money.

Surely, therefore, the trouble must not lie in some unbreachable gulf between the logic of DCF and the nature of CIM but in the poor application of DCF to these investment proposals. Managers need not – and should not – abandon the effort to justify CIM on financial grounds. Instead, they need ways to apply the DCF approach more appropriately and to be more sensitive to the realities and special attributes of CIM.

Technical issues

The DCF approach most often goes wrong when companies set arbitrarily high hurdle rates for evaluating new investment projects. Perhaps they believe that high-return projects can be created by setting high rates rather than by making innovations in product and process technology or by cleverly building and exploiting a competitive advantage in the marketplace. In fact, the discounting function serves only to make cash flows received in the future equivalent to cash flows received now. For this narrow purpose – the only purpose, really, of discounting future cash flows – companies should use a discount rate based on the project's opportunity cost of capital (that is, the return available in the capital markets for investments of the same risk).

It may surprise managers to know that their real cost of capital can be in the neighborhood of 8%. (See Part I of the *Appendix* at the end of the article.) Double-digit hurdle rates that, in part, reflect assumptions of much higher capital costs are considerably wide of the mark. Their discouraging effect on CIM-type investments is not only unfortunate but also unfounded.

Companies also commonly underinvest in CIM and other new process technologies because they fail to evaluate properly all the relevant alternatives. Most of the capital expenditure requests I have seen measure new investments against a status quo alternative of making no new investments – an alternative that usually assumes a continuation of current market share, selling price, and costs. Experience shows, however, that the status quo rarely lasts. Business as usual does not continue undisturbed.

In fact, the correct alternative to new CIM investment should assume a situation of declining cash flows, market share, and profit margins. Once a valuable new process technology becomes available, even if one company decides not to invest in it, the likelihood is that some of its competitors will. As Henry Ford claimed, "If you need a new machine and don't buy it, you pay for it without getting it."[4] (For a more realistic approach to the evaluation of alternatives, see Part II of the *Appendix* at the end of the article.)

A related problem with current practice is its bias toward incremental rather than revolutionary projects. In many companies, the capital approval process specifies different levels of authorization depending on the size of the request. Small investments (under $100,000, say) may need only the approval of the plant manager; expenditures in excess of several million dollars may require the board of directors' approval. This apparently sensible procedure, however, creates an incentive for managers to propose small projects that fall just below the cut-off point where higher level approval would be needed. Over time, a host of little investments, each of which delivers savings in labor, material, or overhead cost, can add up to a less-than-optimal pattern of material flow and to obsolete process technology. (Part III of the *Appendix* shows the consequences of this incremental bias in more detail.)

"I still think 'Buyout' is not a proper name for a dog."

Introducing CIM process technology is not, of course, without its costs. Out-of-pocket equipment expense is only the beginning. Less obvious are the associated software costs that are necessary for CIM equipment to operate effectively. Managers should not be misled by the expensing of these costs for tax and financial reporting purposes into thinking them operating expenses rather than investments. For internal management purposes, software development is as much a part of the investment in CIM equipment as the physical hardware itself. Indeed, in some installations, the programming, debugging, and prototype development may cost more than the hardware.

There are still other initial costs: site preparation, conveyors, transfer devices, feeders, parts orientation, and spare parts for the CIM equipment. Operating and maintenance personnel must be retrained and new operating procedures developed. Like software development, these tax-deductible training and education costs are part of the investment in CIM, not an expense of the periods in which they happen to be incurred.

Further, as some current research has shown, noteworthy declines in productivity often accompany the introduction of new process technology.[5] These productivity declines can last up to a year, even longer when a radical new technology like CIM is installed. Apparently, the new equipment introduces severe and unanticipated process disruptions, which lead to equipment breakdowns that are higher than expected; to operating, repair, and maintenance problems; to scheduling and coordination difficulties; to revised materials standards; and to old-fashioned confusion on the factory floor.

We do not yet know how much of the disruption is caused by inadequate planning. After investing considerable effort and anguish in the equipment acquisition decision, some companies no doubt revert to business as usual while waiting for the new equipment to arrive.

Whatever the cause, the productivity decline is particularly ill timed since it occurs just when a company is likely to conduct a postaudit on whether it is realizing the anticipated savings from the new equipment. Far from achieving anticipated savings, the postaudit will undoubtedly reveal lower output and higher costs than predicted.

Tangible benefits

The usual difficulties in carrying out DCF analysis – choosing an appropriate discount rate and evaluating correctly all relevant investment alternatives – apply with special force to the consideration of investments in CIM process technology. The greater flexibility of CIM technology, which allows it to be used for successive generations of products, gives it a longer useful life than traditional process investments. Because its benefits are likely to persist longer, overestimating the relevant discount rate will penalize CIM investments disproportionately more than shorter lived investments. The compounding effect of excessively high annual interest rates causes future cash flows to be discounted much too severely. Further, if executives arbitrarily specify short payback periods for new investments, the effect will be to curtail more CIM investments than traditional bottleneck-relief projects.

But beyond a longer useful life, CIM technology provides many additional benefits – better quality, greater flexibility, reduced inventory and floor space, lower throughput times, experience with new technology – that a typical capital justification process does not quantify. Financial analyses that focus too narrowly on easily quantified savings in labor, materials, or energy will miss important benefits from CIM technology.

Inventory savings

Some of these omissions can be easily remedied. The process flexibility, more orderly product flow, higher quality, and better scheduling that are typical of properly used CIM equipment will drastically cut both work-in-process (WIP) and finished goods inventory levels. This reduction in average inventory levels represents a large cash inflow at the time the new process equipment becomes operational. This, of course, is a cash savings that DCF analysis can easily capture.

Consider a product line for which the anticipated monthly cost of sales is $500,000. Using existing equipment and technology, the producing division carries about three months of sales in inventory. After investing in flexible automation, the division heads find that reduced waste, scrap, and rework, greater predictability, and faster throughput permit a two-thirds reduction in average inventory levels. (This is not an unrealistic assumption: Murata Machinery Ltd. has reported that its FMS installation permitted a two-thirds reduction in workers, a 450% increase in output, and a 75% cut in inventory levels.[6])

Pruning inventory from three months to one month of sales produces a cash inflow of $1 million in the first year the system becomes operational. If sales increase 10% per year, the company will enjoy increased cash flows from the inventory reductions in all future years too – that is, if the cost of sales rises to $550,000 in the next year, a two-month reduction

Example of an FMS justification analysis

With the following analysis, one U.S. manufacturer of air-handling equipment justified its investment in an FMS installation for producing a key component:

1
Internal manufacture of the component is essential for the division's long-term strategy to maintain its capability to design and manufacture a proprietary product.

2
The component has been manufactured on mostly conventional equipment – some numerically controlled – with an average age of 23 years. To manufacture a product in conformance with current quality specifications, the company must replace this equipment with new conventional equipment or advanced technology.

3
The alternatives are:
Conventional or numerically controlled stand-alone.
Transfer line.
Machining cells.
FMS.

4
FMS compares with conventional technology as Table A shows.

5
Intangible benefits include virtually unlimited flexibility for FMS to modify mix of component models to the exact requirements of the assembly department.

6
The financial analysis for a project life of ten years compares the FMS with conventional technology (static sales assumptions, constant, or base-year, dollars) as Table B shows.

7
With dynamic sales assumptions showing expected increases in production volume, the annual operating savings will double in future years and the financial yield (still using constant, base-year, dollars) will increase to more than 17% per year.

On the basis of this analysis and recognizing the value of the intangible item (5), which had not been incorporated formally, the company selected the FMS option.

Table A

	Conventional equipment	FMS
Utilization	30 %-40 %	80 %-90 %
Number of employees needed (including indirect workers, such as those who do materials handling, inspection, and rework)*	52	14
Reduced scrap and rework	–	$ 60,000 annually
Inventory	$ 2,000,000	$ 1,100,000†
Incremental investment	–	$ 9,200,000

*Each employee costs $36,000 a year in wages and fringe benefits.
†Inventory reductions because of shorter lead times and flexibility.

Table B

Year	Investment	Operating savings	Tax savings ITC and ACRS depreciation	After-tax cash flow 50 %
0	$ 9,200	$ 900‡	$ 920	$ −7,380
1		1,428§	1,311	1,370¶
2		1,428	1,923	1,675
3		1,428	1,835	1,632
4		1,428	1,835	1,632
5		1,428	1,835	1,632
6		1,428		714
7		1,428		714
8		1,428		714
9		1,428		714
10		1,428		714

After-tax yield: 11.1 %.
Payback period: during year 5.

‡$ 900 = Inventory reduction at start of project.

§$ 1,428 = 38 fewer employees at $36,000/year + $60,000 scrap and rework savings.

¶$ 1,370 = (1,428) (1 − 0.50) + (1,311) (0.50).

in inventory saves an additional $100,000 that year, $110,000 the year after, and $121,000 the year after that.

Less floor space

CIM also cuts floor-space requirements. It takes fewer computer-controlled machines to do the same job as a larger number of conventional machines. Also, the factory floor will no longer be used to store inventory. Recall the example of the Japanese plant that installed a flexible manufacturing system and reduced space requirements from 103,000 to 30,000 square feet. These space savings are real, but conventional financial accounting systems do not measure their value well—especially if the building is almost fully depreciated or was purchased years before when price levels were lower. Do not, therefore, look to financial accounting systems for a good estimate of the cost or value of space. Instead, compute the estimate in terms of the opportunity cost of new space: either its square-foot rental value or the annualized cost of new construction.

Many companies that have installed CIM technology have discovered a new factory inside their old one. This new "factory within a factory" occupies the space where excessive WIP inventory and infrequently used special-purpose machines used to sit. Eliminating WIP inventory and rationalizing machine layout can easily lead to savings of more than 50% in floor space. In practice, these savings have enabled some companies to curtail plant and office expansion programs and, on occasion, to fold the operations of a second factory (which could then be sold off at current market prices) into the reorganized original factory.

Higher quality

Greatly improved quality, defined here as conformance to specifications, is a third tangible benefit from investment in CIM technology. Automated process equipment leads directly to more uniform production and, frequently, to an order-of-magnitude decline in defects. These benefits are easy to quantify and should be part of any cash flow analysis. Some managers have seen five- to tenfold reductions in waste, scrap, and rework when they replaced manual operations with automated equipment.

Further, as production uniformity increases, fewer inspection stations and fewer inspectors are required. If automatic gauging is included in the CIM installation, virtually all manual inspection of parts can be eliminated. Also, with 100% continuous automated inspection, out-of-tolerance parts are detected immediately. With manual systems, the entire lot of parts to be produced before a problem is detected would need to be reworked or scrapped.

These capabilities lead, in turn, to significant reductions in warranty expense. When General Electric automated its dishwasher operation, for example, its service call rate fell 50%. Designing manufacturability into products, making the production process more reliable and uniform, and improving automated inspection can all contribute to major cash flow savings. Although it may be hard to estimate these savings out to four or five significant digits, it would be grossly wrong to assume that the benefits are zero. We must overcome the preference of accountants for precision over accuracy, which causes them to ignore benefits they cannot quantify beyond one or two digits of accuracy.

We can estimate still other tangible benefits from CIM. John Shewchuk of General Electric claims that accounts receivable can be reduced by eliminating the incidence of customers who defer payment until quality problems are resolved.[7] Consider too that because improved materials flow can reduce the need for forklift trucks and operators, factories will enjoy a large cash flow saving from not having to acquire, maintain, repair, and operate so many trucks. All these calculations belong in a company's capital justification process.

Intangible benefits

Other benefits of CIM include increased flexibility, faster response to market shifts, and greatly reduced throughput and lead times. These benefits are as important as those just discussed but much harder to quantify. We may not be sure how many zeros should be in our benefits estimate (are they to be measured in thousands or millions of dollars?) much less which digit should be first. The difficulty arises in large part because these benefits represent revenue enhancements rather than cost savings. It is fairly easy to get a ballpark estimate for percentage reductions in costs already being incurred. It is much harder to quantify the magnitude of revenue enhancement expected from features that are not already in place.

Greater flexibility

The flexibility that CIM technology offers takes several forms. The benefits of economies of scope—that is, the potential for low-cost production of high-variety, low-volume goods – are just beginning to flow from FMS environments as early adopters of the technology start to service after-market sales for discontinued models on the same equipment used to produce current high-volume models. We are also beginning to see some customized production on the same lines used for standard products.

Beyond these economy-of-scope applications, CIM's reprogramming capabilities make it possible for machines to serve as backups for each other. Even if a machine is dedicated to a narrow product line, it can still replace lost production during a second or a third shift when a similar piece of equipment, producing quite a different product, breaks down.

Further, by easily accommodating engineering change orders and product redesigns, CIM technology allows for product changes over time. And, if the mix of products demanded by the market changes, a CIM-based process can respond with no increase in costs. The body shop of one automobile assembly plant, for example, quickly adjusted its flexible, programmed spot-welding robots to a shift in consumer preference from the two-door to the four-door version of a certain car model. Had the line been equipped with nonprogrammable welding equipment, the adjustment would have been far more costly.

CIM's flexibility also gives it usefulness beyond the life cycle of the product for which it was purchased. True, in the short run, CIM may perform the same functions as less expensive, inflexible equipment. Many benefits of its flexibility will show up only over time. Therefore, it is difficult to estimate how much this flexibility will be worth. Nonetheless, as we shall see, even an order-of-magnitude estimate may be sufficient.

Shorter throughput & lead time

Another seemingly intangible benefit of CIM is the great reductions it makes possible in throughput and lead time. At the Yamazaki factory described at the beginning of this article, average processing time per work piece fell from 35 to 1.5 days. Other installations, including Yamazaki's Mazak plant in Florence, Kentucky, have reported similar savings, ranging from a low of 50% reduction in processing time to a maximum of nearly 95%. To be sure, some of the benefits from greatly reduced throughput times have already been incorporated in our estimate of savings from inventory reductions. But there is also a no-

table marketing advantage in being able to meet customer demands with shorter lead times and to respond quickly to changes in market demand.

Increased learning

Some investments in new process technology have important learning characteristics. Thus, even if calculations of the net present value of their cash flows turn up negative, the investments can still be quite valuable by permitting managers to gain experience with the technology, test the market for new products, and keep a close watch on major process advances.

These learning effects have characteristics similar to buying options in financial markets. Buying options may not at first seem like a favorable investment, but quite small initial outlays may yield huge benefits down the line. Similarly, were a company to invest in a risky CIM-related project, it could reap big gains should the technology provide unexpected competitive advantages in the future. Moreover, given the rapid pace of technological change and the advantages of being an early market participant, companies that defer process investments until the new technology is well established will find themselves far behind the market leaders. In this context, the decision to defer investment is often a decision not to be a principal player in the next round of product or process innovation.

The companies that in the mid-1970s invested in automatic and electronically controlled machine tools were well positioned to exploit the microprocessor-based revolution in capabilities – much higher performance at much lower cost – that hit during the early 1980s. Because operators, maintenance personnel, and process engineers were already comfortable with electronic technology, it was relatively simple to retrofit existing machines with powerful microelectronics. Companies that had earlier deferred investment in electronically controlled machine tools fell behind: they had acquired no option on these new process technologies.

The bottom line

Although intangible benefits may be difficult to quantify, there is no reason to value them at zero in a capital expenditure analysis. Zero is, after all, no less arbitrary than any other number. Conservative accountants who assign zero values to many intangible benefits prefer being precisely wrong to being vaguely right. Managers need not follow their example.

Author's note: Especially helpful comments on the preliminary draft were made by Robin Cooper and Robert Hayes (Harvard Business School), Alan Kantrow (*Harvard Business Review*), George Kuper (Manufacturing Studies Board), and Scott Richard and Jeff Williams (Carnegie-Mellon).

One way to combine difficult-to-measure benefits with those more easily quantified is, first, to estimate the annual cash flows about which there is the greatest confidence: the cost of the new process equipment and the benefits expected from labor, inventory, floor space, and cost-of-quality savings. If at this point a discounted cash flow analysis—done with a sensible discount rate and a consideration of all relevant alternatives—shows a CIM investment to have a positive net present value, well and good. Even without accounting for the value of intangible benefits, the analysis will have gotten the project over its financial hurdle. If the DCF is negative, however, then it becomes necessary to estimate how much the annual cash flows must increase before the investment does have a positive net present value.

Suppose, for example, that an extra $100,000 per year over the life of the investment is sufficient to give the project the desired return. Then management can decide whether it expects heightened flexibility, reduced throughput and lead times, and faster market response to be worth at least $100,000 per year. Should the company be willing to pay $100,000 annually to enjoy these benefits? If so, it can accept the project with confidence. If, however, the additional cash flows needed to justify the investment turn out to be quite large—say $3 million per year—and management decides the intangible benefits of CIM are not worth that sum, then it is perfectly sensible to turn the investment down.

Rather than attempt to put a dollar tag on benefits that by their nature are difficult to quantify, managers should reverse the process and estimate first how large these benefits must be in order to justify the proposed investment. Senior executives can be expected to judge that improved flexibility, rapid customer service, market adaptability, and options on new process technology may be worth $300,000 to $500,000 per year but, say, $1 million. This may not be exact mathematics, but it does help put a meaningful price on CIM's intangible benefits.

As manufacturers make critical decisions about whether to acquire CIM equipment, they must avoid claims that such investments have to be made on faith alone because financial analysis is too limiting. Successful process investments must yield returns in excess of the cost of capital invested. That is only common sense. Thus the challenge for managers is to improve their ability to estimate the costs and benefits of CIM, not to take the easy way out and discard the necessary discipline of financial analysis.

References

1 This example has appeared in several articles on strategic justification for flexible automation projects. Clifford Young of Arthur D. Little has traced the example to *American Market/Metalworking News*, October 26, 1981. Other examples of the labor, machinery, and throughput savings from flexible manufacturing system installations are presented in Anderson Ashburn and Joseph Jablonowski, "Japan's Builders Embrace FMS," *American Machinist*, February 1985, p. 83.

2 John P. Van Blois, "Economic Models: The Future of Robotic Justification," Thirteenth ISIR/Robots 7 Conference, April 17-21, 1983 (available from Society of Manufacturing Engineers, Dearborn, Michigan).

3 Robert H. Hayes and David A. Garvin, "Managing As If Tomorrow Mattered," HBR May-June 1982, p. 70.

4 Quoted in John Shewchuk, "Justifying Flexible Automation," *American Machinist*, October 1984, p. 93.

5 See Robert H. Hayes and Kim B. Clark, "Exploring the Sources of Productivity Differences at the Factory Level," in *The Uneasy Alliance: Managing the Productivity-Technology Dilemma*, ed. Kim B. Clark, Robert H. Hayes, and Christopher Lorenz (Boston: Harvard Business School Press, 1985), and Bruce Chew, "Productivity and Change: Understanding Productivity at the Factory Level," Harvard Business School Working Paper (1985).

6 "Japan's Builders Embrace FMS," *American Machinist*, February 1985, p. 83.

7 John Shewchuk, "Justifying Flexible Automation."

[See the Appendix on page 78.]

Appendix

Getting the numbers right

Part I
The cost of capital

A company always has the option of repurchasing its common shares or retiring its debt. Therefore, managers can estimate the cost of capital for a project by taking a weighted average of the current cost of equity and debt at the mix of capital financing typical in the industry. Extensive studies of the returns to investors in equity and fixed-income markets during the past 60 years show that from 1926 to 1984 the average total return (dividends plus price appreciation) from holding a diversified portfolio of common stocks was 11.7% per year. This return already includes the effects of rising price levels. Removing the effects of inflation puts the real (after-inflation) return from investments in common stocks at about 8.5% per year (see *Table A*).*

These historical estimates of 8.5% real (or about 12% nominal) are, however, overestimates of the total cost of capital. From 1926 to 1984, fixed-income securities averaged nominal before-tax returns of less than 5% per year. Taking out inflation reduces the real return (or cost) of high-grade corporate debt securities to about 1.5% per year. Even with recent increases in the real interest rate, a mixture of debt and equity financing produces a total real cost of capital of less than 8%.

Many corporate executives will, no doubt, be highly skeptical that their real cost of capital could be 8% or less. Their disbelief probably comes from making one of two conceptual errors, perhaps both. First, executives often attempt to estimate their current cost of capital by looking at their accounting return on investment – that is, the net income divided by the net invested capital – of their divisions or corporations. For many companies this figure can be in the 15% to 25% range.

There are several reasons, however, why an accounting ROI is a poor estimate of a company's real cost of capital. The accounting ROI figure is distorted by financial accounting conventions such as depreciation method and a variety of capitalization and expense decisions. The ROI figure is also distorted by management's failure to adjust both the net income and the invested capital figures for the effects of inflation, an omission that biases the accounting ROI well above the company's actual real return on investment.

The second conceptual error that makes an 8% real cost of capital sound too low is implicitly to compare it with today's market interest rates and returns on common stocks. These rates incorporate expectations of current and future inflation, but the 8.5% historical return on common stocks and the less than 2% return on fixed-income securities are *real* returns, after the effects of inflation have been netted out.

Now it is possible, of course, to do a DCF analysis by using nominal market returns as a way of estimating a company's cost of capital. In fact, this may even be desirable when you are doing an after-tax cash flow analysis since one of the important cash flows being discounted is the nominal tax depreciation shield from new investments. I have, however, seen many a company go seriously wrong by using a nominal discount rate (say in excess of 15%) while it was assuming level cash flows over the life of their investments.

Consider, for example, the data in *Table B*, which is excerpted from an actual capital authorization request. Notice that all the cash flows during the ten years of the project's expected life are expressed in 1977 dollars, even though the company used a 20% discount rate on the cash flows of the several investment alternatives. This assumption of a 20% cost of capital most likely arose from a prior assumption of a real cost of capital of about 10% and an expected inflation

Table A	**Annual return series** 1926-1984		
Mean annual returns			
Series	1926-1984	1950-1984	1975-1984
Common stocks	11.7 %	12.8 %	14.7 %
Long-term corporate bonds	4.7	4.5	8.4
U.S. Treasury bills	3.4	5.1	9.0
Inflation (CPI)	3.2	4.4	7.4
Real annual returns net of inflation			
Series	1926-1984	1950-1984	1975-1984
Common stocks	8.5 %	8.4 %	7.3 %
Long-term corporate bonds	1.5	0.1	1.0
U.S. Treasury bills	0.2	0.6	1.6

rate of 10% per year. But if it believed that inflation would average 10% annually over the life of the project, the company should also have raised the assumed selling price and the unit costs of labor, material, and overhead by their expected price increases over the life of the project.

It is inconsistent to assume a high rate of inflation for the interest rate used in a DCF calculation but a zero rate of price change when you are estimating future net cash flows from an investment. Naturally, this inconsistency – using double-digit discount rates but level cash flows – biases the analysis toward the rejection of new investments, especially those yielding benefits five to ten years into the future. Compounding excessively high interest rates will place a low value on cash flows in these later

years: a 20% interest rate, for example, discounts $1.00 to $.40 in five years and to $.16 in ten years. If companies use discount rates derived from current market rates of return, then they must also estimate rates of price and cost changes for all future cash flows.

Part II
Measuring alternatives

Look again at the capital authorization request in *Table B*. The cash flows from alternative 1 assume a constant level of sales during the next ten years; the cash flows from alternative 5 show a somewhat higher level of sales based on a small increase in market share. The difference in sales revenue as currently projected, however, is not all that great. Only if managers anticipate a steady decrease in market share and sales revenue for alternative 1, a decrease occasioned by domestic or international competitors adopting the new production technology, would alternative 5 show a major improvement over the status quo.

Obviously, not all investments in new process technology are investments that should be made. Even if competitors adopt new technology and profits erode over time, a company may still find that the benefits from investing would not compensate for its costs. But either way, the company should rest its decision on a correct reading of what is likely to happen to cash flows when it rejects a new technology investment.

| Table B | **Example of a capital authorization request*** |

Alternative 1   Rebuild present machines

Year	1977	1978	1979	1980	1981	...	1986
Sales	$ 6,404	$ 6,404	$ 6,404	$ 6,404	$ 6,404	...	$ 6,404
Cost of sales:							
Labor	168	168	168	168	168	...	168
Material	312	312	312	312	312	...	312
Overhead	1,557	1,557	1,557	1,557	1,557	...	1,557

Alternative 5   Purchase all new machines

Year	1977	1978	1979	1980	1981	...	1986
Sales	$ 6,404	$ 6,724	$ 7,060	$ 7,413	$ 7,784	...	$ 7,784
Cost of sales:							
Labor	167	154	148	152	152	...	152
Material	312	328	344	361	380	...	380
Overhead	1,557	1,440	1,390	1,423	1,423	...	1,423

*Adapted from Robert S. Kaplan and Glen Bingham, *Wilmington Tap and Die,* Case 185-124 (Boston: Harvard Business School, 1985).

Part III
Piecemeal investment

Each year, a company or a division may undertake a series of small improvements in its production process – to alleviate bottlenecks, to add capacity where needed, or to introduce islands of automation based on immediate and easily quantified labor savings. Each of these projects, taken by itself, may have a positive net present value. By investing on a piecemeal basis, however, the company or division will never get the full benefit of completely redesigning and rebuilding its plant. Yet the pressures to go forward on a piecemeal basis are nearly irresistible. At any point in time, there are many annual, incremental projects scattered about from which the investment has yet to be recovered. Thus, were management to scrap the plant, its past incremental investments would be shown to be incorrect.

One alternative to this piecemeal approach is to forecast the remaining technological life of the plant and then to enforce a policy of accepting no process improvements that will not be repaid within this period. Managers can treat the money that otherwise would have been invested as if it accrued interest at the company's cost of capital. At the end of the specified period, they could abandon the old facility and build a new one with the latest relevant technology.

Although none of the usual incremental process investments may have been incorrect, the collection of incremental decisions could have a lower net present value than the alternative of deferring most investment during a terminal period, earning interest on the unexpended funds, and then replacing the plant. Again, the failure to evaluate such global investment is not a limitation of

DCF analysis. It is a failure of not applying DCF analysis to all the feasible alternatives to annual, incremental investment proposals.

*Roger G. Ibbotson and Rex A. Sinquefield, *Stocks, Bonds, Bills and Inflation: The Past and the Future* (Charlottesville, Va.: Financial Analysts Research Foundation, 1982). The author has updated this study for returns earned during 1982-1984.

This estimate should be adjusted up or down, depending on whether the project's risk is above or below the risk of the average project in the market. A detailed discussion of appropriate risk adjustments is beyond the scope of this article. Good treatments can be found in David W. Mullins, Jr., "Does the Capital Asset Pricing Model Work?" HBR January-February 1982, p. 105, and in chap. 7-9 in Richard Brealey and Stewart Myers, *Principles of Corporate Finance*, 2d ed. (New York: McGraw-Hill, 1984).

GETTING THINGS DONE

Why live with unfair cost allocations when they're so easy to correct?

Getting Transfer Prices Right: What Bellcore Did

by Edward J. Kovac and Henry P. Troy

The subject of transfer pricing doesn't normally excite many people, but when your transfer pricing system is less than perfect, life gets interesting.

We at Bellcore first got interested in transfer pricing in 1983. That's the year before AT&T was broken up and Bellcore was being formed as the centralized organization supporting the seven regional holding companies. We needed a transfer pricing system to allocate the costs of our research and engineering to Bellcore's client companies. The charge-back system is especially critical for us because our industry is regulated: the local exchange carriers belonging to the seven holding companies that own us must answer to the state utility commissions, which, in turn, want those exchange carriers to get their money's worth from Bellcore. Cross-subsidies are not allowed.

When we designed our charge-back system in 1983, it was state-of-the-art. But within a few years, the system's imperfections began to manifest themselves. For one thing, we had researchers and engineers spending an increasing amount of their time typing documents and making overhead slides because they couldn't abide the high prices the word processing, graphics, technical publications, and secretarial departments were charging. Those in-house departments tried to contain their costs but, in spite of the large work volume, couldn't seem to perform as efficiently as small, independent service companies could. Even as they reduced their work force, costs kept spiraling up.

We studied the situation and found a few places to trim expenses. But improved efficiency was only part of the answer. We eventually discovered that the main problem for certain services lay with our transfer pricing system – specifically, with the way it allocated overhead and rent. Word processing, graphics, technical publications, and secretarial services were paying more than their share. We had to find a fairer way to

distribute overhead and rent charges, which meant tracking what was actually driving them.

Our situation was not unique. Many companies have accounting systems that allocate costs imperfectly. But we've learned that the system can be fine-tuned rather easily, and doing so keeps our transfer pricing mechanism fair and practical.

The bypass problem

When we first devised our charge-back system, we established "service centers" within Bellcore (see the table, "Bellcore's Service Centers"). They run the gamut from records management to the motor pool to secretarial services. Since each of the service organizations not only provided but also consumed services and since cross-subsidies were strictly forbidden, we needed some way for the centers to charge their clients and each other for what they actually used.

Some service centers provide things in measurable units. Charges for these services were easy to allocate because they were based on actual usage. The telecommunications service center, for instance, assesses internal clients and other service centers $17 a month for access to Centrex and assesses toll charges per call, based on usage. Word processing, for another example, charges for each typed page.

Actual usage of the remaining service centers was harder to measure. Travel planning, records management, library services, and the like are not easily quantified. The costs of these nonusage-based service centers were lumped into overhead and assessed to all Bellcore's internal orga-

Edward J. Kovac is division manager, corporate telecommunications at Bellcore (Bell Communications Research). He chaired the committee that investigated Bellcore's transfer pricing system. Henry P. Troy is executive director of Bellcore's account management serving Southwestern Bell. Previously, he was district manager in charge of cost containment and represented the comptroller in recommending changes to the transfer pricing system.

nizations—including other service centers—according to head count.

In the predivestiture Bell system, most managers and researchers never saw the financial impact of, say, using the typing pool or the travel planners. And they assumed that after the divestiture, it would be business as usual. But when fiscal year 1984 came to an end, they were concerned. A typical reaction was: "You mean I spent this much money on graphics, and now I can't hire people or attend conferences?"

It hit them hard again in 1985. It hit them even harder in 1986. By 1987, they were fed up. They said, "The hell with it. I'm going to cut these costs." Their primary targets were the four usage-based service centers, namely, word processing, graphics, technical publications, and secretarial services, whose prices seemed high and arbitrary. They stood to save a lot of money by hiring independent contractors to do the work or by doing it themselves.

A majority of Bellcore employees are scientists, engineers, and mathematicians, most of whom have advanced degrees and are paid accordingly. In 1987, many of them were doing their own word processing and graphics. Others were negotiating with vendors to do the work. This was hardly ideal; the researchers weren't doing what we paid them to do. Also, some of the outside contractors produced low-quality work or charged more than their estimates. And by going outside, we risked the security of our research reports and technical requirements documents.

The bypassed service centers had their hands tied. They were obliged to pass their costs on to a shrinking client base, which drove unit costs up. At one point, typed documents were costing $50 a page. When word processing sent out bills, tempers flared. We knew the situation wasn't right, so we formed a task force to figure out what was going on.

Let them live

Our task force consisted of eight service center managers, two economists from applied research, and a representative of the comptroller's

office. We had three months to make a recommendation about the four troublesome service centers. We considered four basic options.

First, we could do nothing. This option would be painful: morale would slide as jobs dwindled. And it seemed absurd to sit back and watch the people in word processing and graphics lose their jobs while the technical people took time away from the lab to type papers.

The second option was a faster, less painful version of the first: we could dismantle the four service centers. But again, engineers and scientists would have to make their own arrangements to get their clerical work done. If they went outside the company, we might lose control of quality and confidentiality. In addition, the technical organizations didn't want to oversee secretarial and graphics staff. And with many pockets of administrative support staff spread throughout the technical areas, it would be hard to ensure that salaries and promotions were uniform and fair.

Third, we could mandate the use of internal services regardless of price. But the technical organizations didn't like that option and would likely have undermined it.

The final option, the one the task force recommended, was to keep the service centers intact but make the charges reasonable. That meant making whatever changes were necessary to have the work performed internally *and* at a fair price.

The company executives agreed with our recommendation. Now we had to make the four troubled service centers viable. A few members of the original task force continued to meet in an effort to tackle this problem.

Do you get what you pay for?

We had observed that the troubled service centers had something in common: they all relied heavily on people rather than technology. In the computer and data communications centers, for example, personnel represented a small percentage of their budgets; in graphics, word processing, technical publications, and sec-

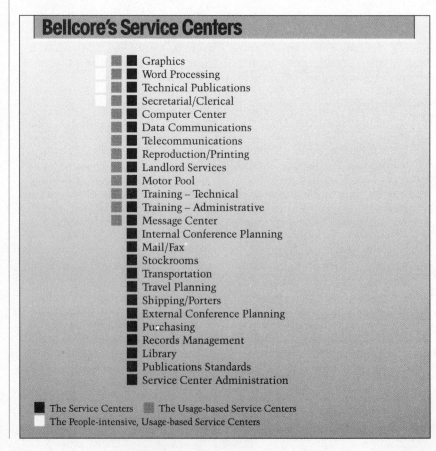

Bellcore's Service Centers

- Graphics
- Word Processing
- Technical Publications
- Secretarial/Clerical
- Computer Center
- Data Communications
- Telecommunications
- Reproduction/Printing
- Landlord Services
- Motor Pool
- Training – Technical
- Training – Administrative
- Message Center
- Internal Conference Planning
- Mail/Fax
- Stockrooms
- Transportation
- Travel Planning
- Shipping/Porters
- External Conference Planning
- Purchasing
- Records Management
- Library
- Publications Standards
- Service Center Administration

■ The Service Centers   ▦ The Usage-based Service Centers
☐ The People-intensive, Usage-based Service Centers

Comparison of Service Center Costs

	4 People-intensive, Usage-based Service Centers	9 Technology-intensive, Usage-based Service Centers
Direct Costs:		
Salaries & Benefits	35%	10%
Equipment Leases & Supplies	10	75
Usage-based Services	12	2
*Nonusage-based Services	12	2
†Landlord Services	16 — 40%	3 — 9%
*General & Administrative	12	4
Capital-related Costs	3	4
Total	100%	100%

*Based on head count †Based on square footage

retarial services, that percentage was much higher. Combined, the four departments represented some 12% of company employment.

The expenses of the four people-intensive service centers varied widely from those of their technology-intensive counterparts (see the table, "Comparison of Service Center Costs"). They spent 35% of their total budget on salaries and benefits; the technology-intensive service centers spent just 10%. They spent another 12% for usage-based services like the computer center and training; the technology-intensive service centers spent 2%.

We went down the list of expenses for the service centers looking for places to trim. At times, we examined their counterparts outside the company for ideas on what to do differently. We found, for instance, that most of the independent word processing and graphics companies had fewer middle managers and administrators, so we suggested that our service centers trim theirs back. We also recommended that they use less centralized computing, which accounted for some of their usage-based expenses. If they bought PCs, they wouldn't have to pay for connect time. We also got them to cut

back on their space and thereby reduce their rent charges for landlord services.

The combined efficiency improvements cut total costs by 12%. That was a step in the right direction, but considering that the independent contractors were charging some 40% less than the in-house providers, it wasn't enough.

We turned our attention to other charges that were much higher than those for the technology-oriented service centers—namely, landlord services, nonusage-based services, and general and administrative services. Combined, these three line items accounted for 40% of the people-intensive service centers' total costs. The comparable figure for technology-intensive service centers was just 9%. We suspected that those costs were distributed unfairly.

That suspicion inevitably brought us to our accounting system. The cost for landlord services was based on the square footage each service center used. The rate per square foot was derived by combining the components of running Bellcore's buildings—maintenance, rent, taxes, utilities—and dividing that number by total square footage. We analyzed the situation as if the people-inten-

sive service centers were independent entities. Would we be able to economize on our rent? The answer was a powerful yes. If we rented the vacant building across the street for our secretaries, for instance, we would cut our expenses for landlord services almost in half. Why, then, did it cost so much to be housed in the building Bellcore occupied?

Bellcore's technical organizations and service centers use space differently. Some require a lot of computer space; others use mostly lab space. The people-intensive service centers use office and open space. It stood to reason that the costs of building and maintaining lab and computer space would be much higher than the costs for open space, and the external real estate market confirmed this. On the open market, lab space was three times as expensive as open offices.

Yet in allocating costs, we lumped all building space together. If certain areas needed tight security or climate control or a 10-inch layer of cables under the floor, the costs were shared among all of Bellcore's service centers. Though the people-intensive service centers needed only open spaces, they were bearing part of the costs of building and maintaining the labs and computer areas. Despite our intentions to avoid cross-subsidies, the people-intensive service centers had in essence been subsidizing the technical organizations' use of space.

Why did in-house graphics cost more than going outside?

Our solution to this problem was a tiered rental rate that takes into account the actual costs of three kinds of building space. With this method, rates for open space dropped 40%; for office space, 30%. Word processing, graphics, technical publications, and clerical services were greatly relieved. Their landlord costs fell by 33%, which meant a 5% reduction in their total costs. Some technical organizations, however, were hard hit. The new system doubled rates for lab

Were the Troubled Service Centers Overcharged?

Nonusage-based Services	Head Count Assessment	Verified Usage
Internal Conference Planning	12%	2%
Mail and Fax Delivery	12	3
Stockrooms	12	3
Transportation Within Bellcore	12	3
Travel Planning	12	1
Shipping and Moving	12	2
External Conference Planning	12	2
Purchasing	12	2
Records Management	12	0
Library	12	1
Publications Standards	12	0
Service Center Administration	12	20

and computer space. These organizations complained loudly, but we've continued to use the new method because we know it is more equitable.

Charges for nonusage-based services (libraries, purchasing, conference planning, and the like) were assessed on the basis of head count. Obviously, the people-intensive service centers were charged proportionately more. But did having more people mean more conferences, more purchase requisitions, more trips to the library?

Probably not. The secretaries don't go on trips. It's the engineers and managers who go to California and Missouri to see their clients. And when do secretaries use the technical library? Rarely. Managers and professional people do. Yet the secretarial and clerical service center was assessed 8% of the costs of those items because it represented 8% of the total work force.

We decided to verify whether these charges were unfair by measuring actual usage. That meant going through the process of counting units—a process that is too tedious to do all the time. We have 11 nonusage-based service centers. We tracked actual usage of each one by measuring whatever unit made the most sense

1. FCC Docket No. 86-111.

for periods of three months to a year. In some cases, we used historical data; in others, we started counting. For the library, we looked at the number of literature searches. For travel planning, we counted the number of trips. For purchasing, we tallied the number of purchase requisitions.

Then we analyzed the numbers. We learned, for example, that the people-intensive service centers ac-

> ## Supervisors—not total head count— drives costs for purchasing and libraries.

counted for only 2% of the conferences that were planned (see the table, "Were the Troubled Service Centers Overcharged?"). They accounted for 1% of the travel plans and 1% of the library searches. Yet they were being charged for 12% of the use of these services because they had 12% of the total head count.

If head count wasn't driving the cost, what was? We considered several possibilities: the percentage of staff at supervisory level or higher, the percentage of technical and ad-

ministrative professionals, and a "general allocator." (The general allocator was a combination of direct costs and capital-related costs, an idea we got from an FCC document.[1] If a service center's direct and capital-related costs were 10% of Bellcore's total, it would be responsible for 10% of overhead.) These alternative allocators were not the only options, but they were logical and available from the accounting system.

To decide which, if any, of them reflected actual use more accurately than head count, we analyzed the variance of the data (see the table, "What Really Drives Costs for Nonusage-based Services?"). The calculations revealed that the proportion of technical and administrative professionals in a department was the best measure of the department's actual usage. That made intuitive sense, since managers and professionals tend to use travel services and libraries much more than clerical workers do.

Since managers and professionals use those services, they should pay for them. If an organization has one-third of all Bellcore's total technical and administrative staff, it should be charged for one-third of the total costs of the nonusage-based services. When we applied this new allocator, the people-intensive service centers cut their costs for nonusage-based services by 75%. That translated into a 9% improvement in their total costs.

We went through a similar process for general and administrative expenses and split them into two categories. For one set of costs (personnel, medical, employee information, and security), total head count was the true cost driver. But for the other set (legal, comptroller, executive), the general allocator was more accurate. These findings confirmed our thinking. Most of our lawyers are doing patent work for the science people. Why should secretaries pay for the lawyers' services? We adjusted the costs accordingly; the result was a 5% reduction in total costs.

Calming the ripples

We had finally gotten to the root of the problem. Word processing, graph-

What Really Drives Costs for Nonusage-based Services?

	Actual Usage	Proposed Allocators Total Head Count	Proportion of Technical & Administrative People	Proportion of People Above Supervisory Level	General Allocator
People-intensive Service Centers	5%	12%	3%	1%	4%
Technology-intensive Service Centers	6	6	5	4	12
Nonusage-based Service Centers	2	4	4	2	2
General and Administrative Services	17	17	17	13	12
Research Organizations	15	11	12	15	12
Development Organizations	55	50	59	65	58
Variance from Actual Usage*		94	34	136	80

*This number is the sum of the squared differences from actual usage. For example, people-intensive service centers actually used 5% of the nonusage-based services. With head count as an allocator, they were charged for 12% of the costs of nonusage-based services. The squared difference is $(5-12)^2$, or 49. The sum of the squared differences is 49 + 0 + 4 + 0 + 16 + 25, or 94. The best allocator is the one with the least variance from actual usage.

ics, technical publications, and secretarial services were losing their corporate customers because they were charging too much. They were charging too much partly because they weren't efficient enough and partly because they were paying more than their share for overhead and rent. The efficiency improvements cut 12% off their total costs, and the new allocation methods cut another 19% (5% for landlord services, 9% for nonusage-based services, and 5% for general and administrative services). The overall cost reduction was 31%.

Implementing the changes was fairly simple. Because our new allo-

An occasional tweak keeps a transfer pricing system up to date.

cators were taken from available data, we had to change only a few lines of computer code for the accounting system. And by the time we had reached that point, the comptroller himself was fully involved and

willing to make whatever changes we recommended.

Smoothing the ripple effects throughout the organization was a delicate matter. To evaluate the effect on all organizations in the company, we did a thorough spreadsheet analysis. In most cases, the impact, whether positive or negative, would be slight. There were, however, a few significant exceptions. As the four targeted service centers' costs went down, other organizations' costs increased. The head of applied research, for example, got an instant $3 million added to his expenses. The company president stood firmly behind our changes, despite the impact on some areas.

Recently, the four people-intensive service centers have been holding their own or expanding, and morale is high. They are being run like small businesses. They have developed business plans that they discuss with other Bellcore managers. They explain what they're planning and ask for feedback.

The other organizations in the company—even those hit the hardest—have slowly accepted the changes. They recognize that the re-

vised system is fairer, especially as the costs for graphics and secretarial services have fallen.

In the process of revising the transfer pricing system, we encountered many skeptics. Some worried that we would make things too complicated; others thought we should abandon the system because it wasn't working. We're glad we didn't throw out the baby with the bathwater.

While there's no question that the transfer pricing mechanism can get extremely complicated, we've learned that simple adjustments can have a big impact on how it functions. Our revised system is only slightly more complex than the old one, and it is much fairer.

We're committed to our transfer pricing system. We want to preserve it, and that means we'll occasionally have to tweak it. As long as we keep our heads out of the sand, we'll know when it's time to do the fine-tuning: when good managers complain loudly or act illogically. We have no doubt that the system will get better with each round.

Reprint 89507

Getting Things Done

When is there cash in cash flow?

James McNeill Stancill

Any company, no matter how big or small, moves on cash, not profits. You can't pay bills with profits, only cash. You can't pay employees with profits, only cash. And when anyone asks you, "Did you make any profits?" all they probably want to know is whether you've got any cash.

Those may sound like extreme statements, but time and again I've heard managers complain, "If I'm making such big profits, why don't I have any money?" It doesn't matter whether your industry is high tech or low, smokestack or service. In the end, you need to have enough money to pay your obligations or you'll go out of business.

Emphasizing the importance of cash is not a new idea, of course. I've written about it many times; others have given cash flow the status of a new religion. Still others are heretics or wedded to the ideas of the old church. Whatever the debates of academics, managers are—as always—caught. It seems they have either too much cash or not enough.

As a teacher and consultant, I have heard many executives explain

Mr. Stancill is professor of finance at the University of Southern California's Graduate School of Business. An expert in the financing of growing companies, he has contributed many articles to HBR, including "How Much Money Does Your New Venture Need?" (May-June 1986).

how they get caught and why. One reason is that the usual measures of cash flow—net income plus depreciation (NIPD) or earnings before interest and taxes (EBIT)—give a realistic indication of a company's cash position only during a period of steady sales. That's because both are based on the company's income statement and don't include working-capital items—principally, accounts receivable, inventory, and accounts payable.

> *You can't pay bills with profits— only cash.*

For that reason, when the corporate pendulum swings in the direction of faster sales or impending recession, these measures may make it seem as if a company has more cash or less cash than it really does. That may prove disastrous when you're trying to decide whether to take on more debt obligations or trying to meet the ones you've already got.

It seemed to me that a measure was needed to tell managers what their bottom cash line really was—how much money they had (or, when modeling for future scenarios, would have) to pay debts before spending on "frills"

like R&D and capital expenditures. Called net operating cash flow—double prime (NOCF″)—the measure I developed shows the absolute minimum cash necessary for a company to service its debt.

In this article, I will show first how I derived NOCF″ from a cash flow statement and then how you can use it in a model to predict your company's true cash flow picture under a steady sales scenario or explosive growth and during a recession.

The cash flows in

To project your capital requirements, you can use a cash flow statement like the one opposite. The statement's first three sections (operating cash inflows, operating cash outflows, and net operating cash flow) deal with the company's basic operations. If you subtract the operating cash outflows from the operating cash inflows, you get net operating cash flow (NOCF)—the amount of money a company has to do things.

The next three sections detail what those things might be. The first is to pay interest and debt (priority outflows); the second, capital expenditures, R&D, and dividends (discretionary outflows); and the third, sale or repurchase of stock or term loans (financial flows). Periodic repayments of these loans come under the priority outflows section. The sum total of the statement, the net change in cash and marketable securities, is the amount of cash the company has left over.

What's interesting about this statement is that two models can be derived from it to answer important questions that all managers ask: How much money will I have for my discretionary outflows (capital expenditures and dividends)? How much money will I have to service my debt? To answer these questions, we have to begin with NOCF—that is, how much money do I have from the company's basic operations with which I can do things?

If you subtract priority outflows from NOCF, you get the first model, NOCF′—or the amount of money available for discretionary outflows. I call this the amount of money to "plow back or pay out."

Sample cash flow statement

Cash flow statement for the period _____ to _____

		Month			
Operating cash inflows	+ Net sales	$	$	$	$
	+ Other income				
	− Δ Accounts receivable				
	1 Net operating cash inflows	$	$	$	$
Operating cash outflows	+ Cost of goods sold less depreciation	$	$	$	$
	+ General and administrative expenses				
	+ Selling expenses				
	+ Taxes				
	− Δ Accrued taxes				
	+ Δ Inventory				
	+ Δ Prepaid expenses				
	− Δ Accounts payable				
	2 Total operating cash outflows	$	$	$	$
	3 Net operating cash flow (Item 1 less item 2)	$	$	$	$
Priority outflows	+ Interest expenses	$	$	$	$
	+ Current debt repayable				
	+ Lease payments (not included above)				
	4 Total priority outflows	$	$	$	$
Discretionary outflows	+ Capital expenditures	$	$	$	$
	+ Research and development expenses				
	+ Preferred stock dividends				
	+ Common stock dividends				
	5 Total discretionary outflows	$	$	$	$
Financial flows	+ Δ Debt instruments (borrowings)	$	$	$	$
	+ Δ Stock securities (equity)				
	+ Δ Term loans				
	6 Total financial flows	$	$	$	$
Net change in cash and marketable securities accounts	+ Net operating cash flow (item 3)	$	$	$	$
	− Priority outflows (item 4)				
	− Discretionary outflows (item 5)				
	+ Financial flows (item 6)				
	7 Net change in cash and marketable securities	$	$	$	$
End-of-period cash balance		$	$	$	$

Δ = Period-to-period change in total dollar amount

The second model—with which I will deal in this article—is also based on NOCF and is called NOCF''. If you allocated all of NOCF to priority outflows, you would have no money left for even a "bare bones" capital budgeting program or certain minimum dividends. I call these minimum amounts "necessary discretionary outflows," or $_{nec}$Discretionary. Therefore

$$NOCF'' = NOCF - {}_{nec}Discretionary$$

In other words, this is the amount of money you will have to service your debt.

The "prime" and "double prime" are not used to be clever or different for difference's sake; rather, they point out a very important fact about a cash flow statement: everything starts with NOCF. Prime and double prime also show the circular nature of the problem; the more priority outflows you have, the less you have available for discretionary outflows, and the more you want in your necessary discretionary category, the less you have available for priority outflows.

Under steady sales

When a company enjoys steady sales, all's right with the world and all's right with each of the cash flow indicators we're going to review—NIPD, EBIT, and NOCF''. They reflect reality. In fact, periods of steady growth make a good starting point from which to explore the impact of more dramatic situations (like rapid growth or recession) on cash flow. So I began running simulations for three types of companies—a manufacturing company (machine tools), a wholesale company (paper merchant), and a service company (wholesale laundry)—and at first allowed their sales to vary up or down by no more than 5%.

The graphs throughout this article give the simulation results. They show the assumptions made for the particular scenario, the six-year sales progression (shown on the horizontal axis of each graph in 12 6-month intervals because bond interest is paid that way), the three cash flow mea-

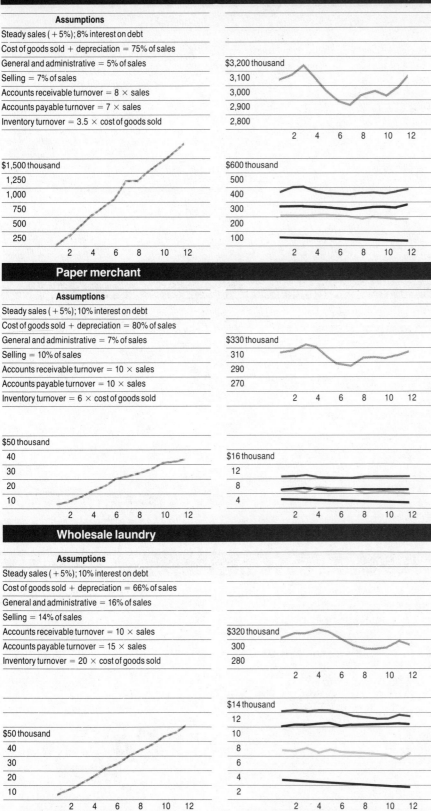

When growth is steady and sure

Machine tool manufacturer

Assumptions
Steady sales (+ 5%); 8% interest on debt
Cost of goods sold + depreciation = 75% of sales
General and administrative = 5% of sales
Selling = 7% of sales
Accounts receivable turnover = 8 × sales
Accounts payable turnover = 7 × sales
Inventory turnover = 3.5 × cost of goods sold

Paper merchant

Assumptions
Steady sales (+ 5%); 10% interest on debt
Cost of goods sold + depreciation = 80% of sales
General and administrative = 7% of sales
Selling = 10% of sales
Accounts receivable turnover = 10 × sales
Accounts payable turnover = 10 × sales
Inventory turnover = 6 × cost of goods sold

Wholesale laundry

Assumptions
Steady sales (+ 5%); 10% interest on debt
Cost of goods sold + depreciation = 66% of sales
General and administrative = 16% of sales
Selling = 14% of sales
Accounts receivable turnover = 10 × sales
Accounts payable turnover = 15 × sales
Inventory turnover = 20 × cost of goods sold

Cash flow measures
Sales; Cash balance; EBIT; NIPD; NOCF''; Priority

sures, and the cash balance that would result if the particular company used cash for nothing but minimum capital spending.

Under the steady sales scenario to the left, the difference between EBIT and NIPD is the amount of taxes paid. Discretionary outflows (for capital spending, R&D, and dividend payments) separate NIPD and NOCF''.

Notice that in the cases of the machine tool manufacturer and the paper merchant, NIPD almost equals NOCF'' because there is little or no net change in working capital (including accounts receivable, inventory, accounts payable, and accrued taxes). If you removed these working-capital items from items one and two on the cash flow statement, only the items on the income statement would remain. Indeed, when sales neither rise nor fall appreciably, a business shouldn't need any increase in working capital. The *net change* on the balance sheet working-capital items should be about zero. Under this scenario, NOCF'' is an income statement concept – but only under this scenario!

Because each company will have more cash to pay its debt than its debt service requires (NOCF'' exceeds priority outflows), the model predicts that the companies' cash balances will steadily rise over time. In reality, of course, a business would never let its cash and marketable securities balance increase constantly. But right now I am not interested in too much reality; I want to show what might happen to cash flow given certain assumptions.

Looking more closely at the paper merchant, the similarity between NIPD and NOCF'' becomes even more apparent than in the case of the machine tool producer. The two measures are roughly equal because the wholesale outfit spends very little on capital projects or R&D. The changes in working capital remain near zero.

Because the working-capital requirements stay about the same, NIPD gives you a fair estimate of cash flow and NOCF'' under steady sales. You can trace any cash increase directly to the differences between what a company owes and what it has to repay the debt. If a company has a large debt-service obligation, the cash balance will rise more slowly. If it reduces its debt, the balance will rise faster.

Avoiding the perils of growth

When a company starts to grow faster than expected, NIPD and EBIT are of little use. They do not measure reality. NOCF'', on the other hand, does. Measuring it can help management cope with some of the peculiarities that might result.

Consider the graphs on the right. When I let the machine tool maker's sales go up by 20% annually over six years, the results are dramatic. EBIT and NIPD rise accordingly; you can just imagine the ecstatic manufacturing managers describing their cash flow picture as "great." But they should look at NOCF''. Right from the start, that measure declines and finally pushes the company into the red. That's why its cash balances turn downward. (Recall that this is only a simulation. Obviously, no bank would allow a customer to overdraw consistently for six years—or no bank that I know of).

You can turn these results around to help answer the obvious question that arises. If the company does not have enough cash to finance such desirable growth, then how much cash would it need? It cannot finance the growth internally. And things would only be worse if its debt service increased (I have assumed no debt service at all).

Answering that question requires you to take a look at what I like to call the company's "hot buttons." Imagine yourself sitting before a console with buttons for the following items in front of you—gross profit, turnover of receivables, inventory, and accounts payable.

Growing tall and growing long

Machine tool manufacturer

Assumptions
Sales increasing at 20% a year
Cost of goods sold + depreciation = 75% of sales
General and administrative = 5% of sales
Selling = 7% of sales
Accounts receivable turnover = 8 × sales
Accounts payable turnover = 7 × sales
Inventory turnover = 3 × cost of goods sold

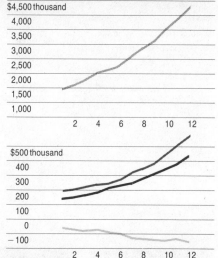

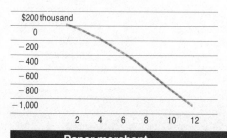

Paper merchant

Assumptions
Sales increasing at 25% a year from period 4
Cost of goods sold + depreciation = 80% of sales
General and administrative = 7% of sales
Selling = 10% of sales
Accounts receivable turnover = 10 × sales
Accounts payable turnover = 10 × sales
Inventory turnover = 6 × cost of goods sold

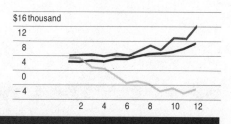

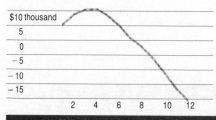

Wholesale laundry

Assumptions
Sales increasing at 25% a year from period 4
Cost of goods sold + depreciation = 66% of sales
General and administrative = 16% of sales
Selling = 14% of sales
Accounts receivable turnover = 10 × sales
Accounts payable turnover = 15 × sales
Inventory turnover = 20 × cost of goods sold

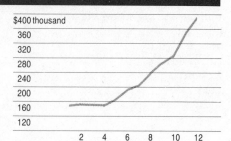

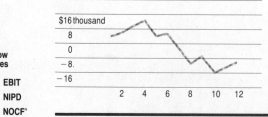

Cash flow measures	
Sales	EBIT
Cash balance	NIPD
	NOCF''

These four variables have a dramatic effect on a company's cash flow. They are the principal reason one company differs from another, or companies in one industry differ from companies in other industries. Companies with large gross profits and very fast inventory and receivables turnovers generate a lot of cash and could self-finance substantial growth. Conversely, companies with anemic gross profits and slow turnovers of accounts receivable and/or inventory find that even a little growth needs external financing. So the trick to financial management is how you handle these hot buttons—within the constraints of your company and industry.

Let's make a change, for example, in the assumption about the cost of goods sold, accounts receivable, and inventory. If you change the cost of goods sold, you can improve the company's projected cash flow. As shown on the right, I assumed different values for the machine tool maker's cost of goods sold, ranging from 70% to 78%. Taking out just two percentage points saves several hundred thousand dollars over the the course of the planning period. Conversely, if management gets careless and lets the cost of goods sold slip to 78%, it would need 33% more cash to finance this growth. And if it could reduce the cost of goods sold to something less than 70%, it could self-finance a 20% growth rate.

Now look at the button marked "accounts receivable." I first let accounts receivable turnover slow down to six turns. Then I speeded up collections so that it became ten turns over the same period. The cumulative effect was not dramatic—something like $100,000 to $200,000 over the six-year period. (As a cash flow fanatic, I was surprised by this result but not persuaded that varying accounts receivable wouldn't help some company sometime. You have to simulate the cash flow in each case to see what impact a certain change might have.)

Pushing the button marked "inventory" had more exciting results. Under the first scenario, I assumed a slow three turns in inventory each year. If, through better inventory management, you could increase the turnover to 4.5 times a year, you could make the six-year trip of 20% growth on half the financing.

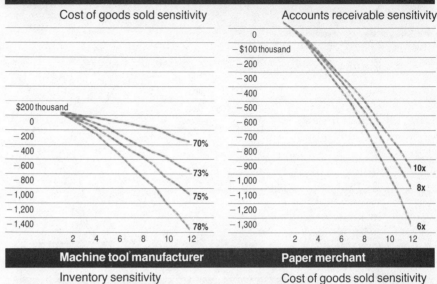

Pushing new buttons

Machine tool manufacturer
Cost of goods sold sensitivity

Accounts receivable sensitivity

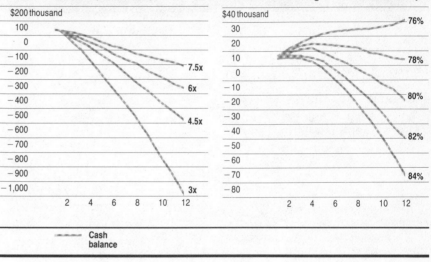

Machine tool manufacturer
Inventory sensitivity

Paper merchant
Cost of goods sold sensitivity

Cash balance

Getting it wholesale

As you can see, this model allows you to test just what rate of sales growth you can finance internally—or how much growth you should strive for given the external financing available. In the case of the paper merchant, for example, I let sales stay steady for four half-year periods and then rise 25% annually. NIPD and NOCF'' stay rather close at first, but as soon as sales start climbing, NIPD goes up and NOCF'' goes down. The cash balance reflects this decline—it rises under steady sales and falls as soon as growth stops.

How could the paper merchant change the outcome? As shown above, I originally assumed the cost of goods sold to be 80%. If the company takes only two percentage points out of the cost of goods sold, it could self-finance a 25% growth rate. Conversely, a cost of goods sold of 84% would require three times as much financing. I deliberately did not touch any one of the other hot buttons in this case. The company might be able to cut prices if it buys in large lots, but what would happen to inventory turnover and cash balance?

Going down, ringing up

Machine tool manufacturer

Assumptions

25% decrease in sales; 8% interest on debt

Period	1-4	5	6	7	8	9-12
CGS + dep.	.75	.78	.83	.80	.76	.75
A/R turn.	8	7.5	7	7	7.5	8
A/P turn.	8	7.5	7	7	7.5	8
Inv. turn.	4 × CGS					

SG&A decreases less rapidly than sales

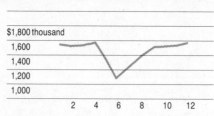

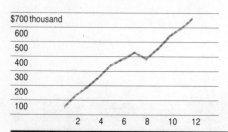

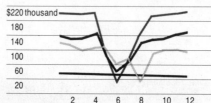

Paper merchant

Assumptions

30% decrease in sales; 10% interest on debt

Period	1-4	5	6	7	8	9-12
CGS + dep.	.8	.82	.83	.82	.81	.80
A/R turn.	10	9.5	9	8.5	9	10
A/P turn.	10	9.5	9	8.5	9	10
Inv. turn.	6	5.75	5.5	5.25	5.5	6

SG&A decreases less rapidly than sales

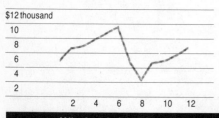

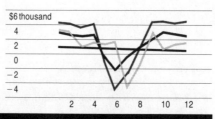

Wholesale laundry

Assumptions

25% decrease in sales; 10% interest on debt

Period	1-4	5	6	7	8	9-12
CGS + dep.	.66	.69	.72	.70	.68	.66
A/R turn.	15	14	13	13	14	15
A/P turn.	10	9.5	9	9	9.5	10
Inv. turn.	20	19	18	18	19	20

SG&A decreases less rapidly than sales

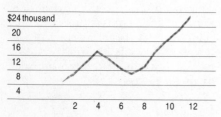

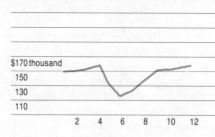

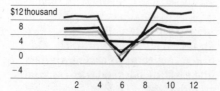

When I let the wholesale laundry's sales increase rapidly, the results were similar to the paper merchant's. However, because the service company carries little inventory, the same rate of growth would require less additional cash. When I tested the cost of goods sold, I found that the laundry could self-finance at 64%; at 68% it would need a modest amount of capital. I also found that the company could self-finance at an accounts receivable turn of 12 times.

Going down, ringing up

I recently gave a talk on cash flow to an industry trade group association and let one of my sample companies run out of cash—and crash. One manager, dissenting from my bleak scenario, reported that he had never had as much cash as at the end of the last recession. This often happens in an economic downturn. When I put the three companies through a recession, they all came out with more cash at its end than they had had at its beginning.

This unexpected result occurs, in part, because I assumed that good managers would react quickly and run a tight ship. As the graphs on the left show, I assumed that the full drop in sales (25% for the machine tool maker and the wholesale laundry and 30% for the paper merchant) came during the fifth and sixth periods while good management brought about a recovery over 1½ years. Management accomplished this by, for example, keeping key people who could push the company's growth back up once it had bottomed out. I reflected this assumption by increasing the cost of goods sold percentage relative to sales as sales declined but not in the same proportion. Good managers will hold on to key subordinates despite falling sales; laying them off without regard to their potential importance in an upswing would be foolhardy.

In the same way, I assumed that the "indirect overhead" portion of the cost of goods sold would remain fixed (you can't do much about rent and depreciation no matter what the economic weather). That puts upward pressure on the cost of goods sold. I slowed the turnover ratios of accounts receivable and accounts payable and held the inventory turnover constant for manufacturing while allowing it to fall for the wholesale and service companies. SG&A would also decrease, although not as fast as sales.

Looking at the model of the machine tool maker, you can see sales start to drop after the fourth period. Since NOCF'' exceeds the priority outflows at the same time, the cash balance rises. As sales start to decline, both EBIT and NIPD also fall but at a faster rate because of the financial and operating leverage used. As sales start up, EBIT and NIPD respond in kind before leveling off.

NOCF'' is not tied strictly to sales, however, and does not mirror its movement. When sales decline in the fifth period, NOCF'' actually goes up slightly before falling at a slower rate because the company is running off its receivables and inventory. As a result, NOCF'' is greater than EBIT or NIPD in the recession's trough.

When sales start up, NOCF'' increases at first but then declines, hitting its trough in the eighth period, one year after the more popular measures of cash flow bottom out. The reason that the cash balance is higher at the end of the recession than at the beginning is that the company cut the cost of goods sold and SG&A expenses decisively and punctually. If management had reacted more slowly, the company would have wasted more cash. And if the company's debt service were greater, NOCF'' would dip below priority outflows and would decrease the cash balance.

For the paper merchant and laundry, I assumed a higher level of debt service. So when sales dipped, NOCF'' remained strong before dropping. This

Author's note: I wish to thank Mohammed Najam for his research assistance. This article is dedicated to him. I also wish to thank James Walter, who developed the basic cash flow statement I use and who got me interested in cash flow analysis.

Trying another button

Machine tool manufacturer

Accounts receivable sensitivity

Period	1-4	5	6	7	8	9-12
1	8	7	6.5	6.5	7	8
2	8	6.75	6	6	6.75	8
3	8	6	5.5	5.5	6	8

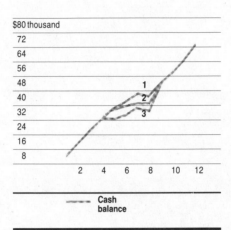

— — — Cash
balance

phenomenon is more marked in the case of the paper merchant because it has a large inventory it can deplete. Because priority outflows are closer to NOCF'', when NOCF'' goes below that low-water mark, the cash balance declines for several periods before starting back up.

It's easy to think you've got cash when you don't.

Next I varied the turnover in accounts receivable. If you've ever wondered whether there's any cash in accounts receivable, here is your proof. Looking at the graph above, as sales start to drop for the manufacturing company, the three different accounts receivable turnover rates affect the cash balance in different ways. Most interesting, however, is the fact that the cash balance returns to the same amount when the accounts receivable turnover rates also become equal.

Paying bills with real money

It takes cash, not earnings, to pay interest and repay debt. Except under the most idealized steady sales situation, you need a more reliable measure of cash flow to predict whether you can pay these obligations. I want to caution you, however, not to try to memorize the cash flow patterns I have described here. They will change depending on the key assumptions used— what I called the "hot buttons."

In looking at the manufacturing company during a recession, for example, the cash balance was greater at the end of the recession than at its beginning because of the company's excellent financial and asset management. For you to conclude that you have nothing to fear from a recession, however, would naturally be a mistake. When sales bottom out, you won't necessarily be flush with cash. Conversely, in a growth scenario, it is foolish to think that you will have plenty of cash just because NIPD or EBIT looks great. You have to investigate your own circumstances to draw your own conclusions. I hope this article has begun to show you how. ▽

Reprint 87211

The Performance Measurement Manifesto

by Robert G. Eccles

Revolutions begin long before they are officially declared. For several years, senior executives in a broad range of industries have been rethinking how to measure the performance of their businesses. They have recognized that new strategies and competitive realities demand new measurement systems. Now they are deeply engaged in defining and developing those systems for their companies.

At the heart of this revolution lies a radical decision: to shift from treating financial figures as the foundation for performance measurement to treating them as one among a broader set of measures. Put like this, it hardly sounds revolutionary. Many managers can honestly claim that they – and their companies – have tracked quality, market share, and other nonfinancial measures for years. Tracking these measures is one thing. But giving them equal (or even greater) status in determining strategy, promotions, bonuses, and other rewards is another. Until that happens, to quote Ray Stata, the CEO of Analog Devices, "When conflicts arise, financial considerations win out."[1]

The ranks of companies enlisting in this revolution are rising daily. Senior managers at one large,

high-tech manufacturer recently took direct responsibility for adding customer satisfaction, quality, market share, and human resources to their formal measurement system. The impetus was their realization that the company's existing system, which was largely financial, undercut its strategy, which focused on customer service. At a smaller manufacturer, the catalyst was a leveraged recapitalization that gave the CEO the opportunity formally to reorder the company's priorities. On the new list, earnings per share dropped to last place, preceded by customer satisfaction, cash flow, manufacturing effectiveness, and innovation (in that order). On the old list, earnings per share stood first and almost alone.

In both companies, the CEOs believe they have initiated a sea change in how their managers think about business performance and in the decisions they make. Executives at other companies engaged in comparable efforts feel the same – rightly. What gets measured gets attention, particularly when rewards are tied to the measures. Grafting new measures onto

Robert Eccles is a professor of business administration at the Harvard Business School. This article grows out of research and course development for a new first-year course, "Information, Organization, and Control."

---

1. Ray Stata, "Organizational Learning – The Key to Management Innovation," *Sloan Management Review*, Spring 1989, pp. 63-74.

an old accounting-driven performance system or making slight adjustments in existing incentives accomplishes little. Enhanced competitiveness depends on starting from scratch and asking: "Given our strategy, what are the most important measures of performance?" "How do these measures relate to one another?" "What measures truly predict long-term financial success in our businesses?"

Dissatisfaction with using financial measures to evaluate business performance is nothing new. As far back as 1951, Ralph Cordiner, the CEO of General Electric, commissioned a high-level task force to identify key corporate performance measures. (The categories the task force singled out were timeless and comprehensive: in addition to profitability, the list included market share, productivity, employee attitudes, public responsibility, and the balance between short- and long-term goals.) But the current wave of discontent is not just more of the same.

One important difference is the intensity and nature of the criticism directed at traditional accounting systems. During the past few years, academics and practitioners have begun to demonstrate that accrual-based performance measures are at best obsolete – and more often harmful.[2] Diversity in products, markets, and business units puts a big strain on rules and theories developed for smaller, less complex organizations. More dangerously, the numbers these systems generate often fail to support the investments in new technologies and markets that are essential for successful performance in global markets.

Such criticisms reinforce concern about the pernicious effects of short-term thinking on the competitiveness of U.S. companies. Opinions on the causes of this mind-set differ. Some blame the investment community, which presses relentlessly for rising quarterly earnings. Others cite senior managers themselves, charging that their typically short tenure fosters shortsightedness. The important

> ## Managers' willingness to play the earning game calls into question the very measures the market focuses on.

point is that the mind-set exists. Ask almost any senior manager and you will hear about some company's failure to make capital investments or pursue long-term strategic objectives that would imperil quarterly earnings targets.

Moreover, to the extent that managers do focus on reported quarterly earnings – and thereby reinforce the investment community's short-term perspective and expectations – they have a strong incentive to manipulate the figures they report. The extent and severity of such gaming is hard to document. But few in management deny that it goes on or that managers' willingness to play the earnings game calls into question the very measures the market focuses on to determine stock prices. For this reason, many managers, analysts, and financial economists have begun to focus on cash flow in the belief that it reflects a company's economic condition more accurately than its reported earnings do.[3]

Finally, many managers worry that income-based financial figures are better at measuring the consequences of yesterday's decisions than they are at indicating tomorrow's performance. Events of the past decade substantiate this concern. During the 1980s, many executives saw their companies' strong financial records deteriorate because of unnoticed declines in quality or customer satisfaction or because global competitors ate into their market share. Even managers who have not been hurt feel the need for preventive action. A senior executive at one of the large money-center banks, for example, grew increasingly uneasy about the European part of his business, its strong financials notwithstanding. To address that concern, he has nominated several new measures (including customer satisfaction, customers' perceptions of the bank's stature and professionalism, and market share) to serve as leading indicators of the business's performance.

Discontent turns into rebellion when people see an alternative worth fighting for. During the 1980s, many managers found such an alternative in the quality movement. Leading manufacturers and service providers alike have come to see quality as a strategic weapon in their competitive battles. As a result, they have committed substantial resources to developing measures such as defect rates, response time, delivery commitments, and the like to evaluate the performance of their products, services, and operations.

In addition to pressure from global competitors, a major impetus for these efforts has been the growth of the Total Quality Movement and related programs such as the Malcolm Baldrige National Quality Award. (Before a company can even apply for a Baldrige Award, it must devise criteria to measure the performance of its entire operation – not just its products – in minute detail.) Another impetus, getting stronger by the day, comes from large manufacturers who are more and more likely to impose rigid quality requirements on their suppliers. Whatever the stimulus, the result is the same: quality measures represent the most positive step taken to date in broadening the basis of business performance measurement.

Another step in the same direction comes from embryonic efforts to generate measures of customer satisfaction. What quality was for the 1980s, customer satisfaction will be for the 1990s. Work on this class of measures is the highest priority at the two manufacturing companies discussed earlier. It is equally critical at another high-tech company that recently created a customer satisfaction department reporting directly to the CEO. In each case, management's interest in developing new performance measures was triggered by strategies emphasizing customer service.

As competition continues to stiffen, strategies that focus on quality will evolve naturally into strategies based on customer service. Indeed, this is already happening at many leading companies. Attention to customer satisfaction, which measures the quality of customer service, is a logical next step in the development of quality measures. Companies will continue to measure quality on the basis of internally generated indexes (such as defect rates) that are presumed to relate to customer satisfaction. But they will also begin to evaluate their performance by collecting data directly from customers for more direct measures like customer retention rates, market share, and perceived value of goods and services.

Just as quality-related metrics have made the performance measurement revolution more real, so has the development of competitive benchmarking.[4] First, benchmarking gives managers a methodology that can be applied to any measure, financial or nonfinancial, but that emphasizes nonfinancial metrics. Second (and less obvious), it has a transforming effect on managerial mind-sets and perspectives.

Benchmarking involves identifying competitors and/or companies in other industries that exemplify best practice in some activity, function, or process and then comparing one's own performance to theirs. This externally oriented approach makes people aware of improvements that are orders of magnitude beyond what they would have thought possible. In contrast, internal yardsticks that measure current performance in relation to prior period results, current budget, or the results of other units within the company rarely have such an eye-opening effect. Moreover, these internally focused comparisons have the disadvantage of breeding complacency through a false sense of security and of stirring up more energy for intramural rivalry than for competition in the marketplace.

Finally, information technology has played a critical role in making a performance measurement revolution possible. Thanks to dramatically improved price-performance ratios in hardware and to breakthroughs in software and database technology, organizations can generate, disseminate, analyze, and store more information from more sources, for more people, more quickly and cheaply than was conceivable even a few years back. The potential of new technologies, such as hand-held computers for employees in the field and executive information systems for senior managers, is only beginning to be explored. Overall, the range of measurement options that are economically feasible has radically increased.

Veterans know it is easier to preach revolution than to practice it. Even the most favorable climate can create only the potential for revolutionary change. Making it happen requires conviction, careful preparation, perseverance, and a decided taste for ambiguity. As yet, there are no clear-cut answers or predetermined processes for managers who wish to change their measurement systems. Based on the experience of companies engaged in this revolution, I can identify five areas of activity that sooner or later need to be addressed: developing an information architecture; putting the technology in place to support this architecture; aligning incentives with the new system; drawing on outside resources; and designing a process to ensure that the other four activities occur.

Developing a new information architecture must be the first activity on any revolutionary agenda. Information architecture is an umbrella term for the categories of information needed to manage a company's businesses, the methods the company uses to generate this information, and the rules regulating its flow. In most companies, the accounting system implicitly defines the information architecture. Other performance measures are likely to be informal – records that operating managers keep for themselves, for instance – and they are rarely integrated into the corporate-driven financial system.

The design for a new corporate information architecture begins with the data that management needs to pursue the company's strategy. This may sound like a truism, but a surprising number of companies describe their strategies in terms of customer service, innovation, or the quality and capabilities of

2. Donald A. Curtis, "The Modern Accounting System," *Financial Executive*, January-February 1985, pp. 81-93; and H. Thomas Johnson and Robert S. Kaplan, *Relevance Lost* (Boston: Harvard Business School Press, 1987).

3. Yuji Ijiri, "Cash Flow Accounting and Its Structure," *Journal of Accounting, Auditing, and Finance*, Summer 1978, pp. 331-348.

4. Robert C. Camp, *Benchmarking* (Milwaukee, Wisconsin: ASQS Quality Press, 1989).

their people, yet do little to measure these variables. Even time – the newest strategic variable – remains largely underdeveloped in terms of which time-based metrics are most important and how best to measure them.

As part of this identification process, management needs to articulate a new corporate grammar and define its own special vocabulary – the basic terms that will need to be common and relatively invariant across all the company's businesses. Some of these terms (like sales and costs) will be familiar. Others, however, will reflect new strategic priorities and ways to think about measuring performance. For example, both a large money-center bank and a multidivisional, high-technology manufacturer introduced the use of cross-company customer identification numbers so they could readily track such simple and useful information as the total amount of business the company did with any one customer. It sounds elementary and it is – as soon as you start to look at the entire measurement system from scratch.

Uniformity can be carried too far. Different businesses with different strategies require different information for decision making and performance measurement. But this should not obscure the equally obvious fact that every company needs to have at least a few critical terms in common. Today few large companies do. Years of acquisitions and divestitures, technological limitations, and at times, a lack of management discipline have all left most big organizations with a complicated hodgepodge of definitions and variables – and with the bottom line their only common denominator.

Developing a coherent, companywide grammar is particularly important in light of an ever-more stringent competitive environment. For many companies, ongoing structural reorganizations are a fact of life. The high-technology company described above has reorganized itself 24 times in the past 4 years (in addition to a number of divisional and functional restructurings) to keep pace with changes in its mar-

> One high-tech company has reorganized 24 times in the past 4 years to keep pace with changes in its markets.

kets and technologies. Rather than bewail the situation, managers relish it and see their capacity for fast adaptation as an important competitive advantage.

A common grammar also enhances management's ability to break apart and recombine product lines and market segments to form new business units. At a major merchant bank, for example, the organization is so fluid that one senior executive likens it to a collection of hunting packs that form to pursue business opportunities and then disband as the market windows on those opportunities close. The faster the company can assemble information for newly formed groups, the greater the odds of success. So this executive (who calls himself the czar of information) has been made responsible for developing standard definitions for key information categories.

How a company generates the performance data it needs is the second piece of its information architecture. Not surprisingly, methods for measuring financial performance are the most sophisticated and the most deeply entrenched. Accountants have been refining these methods ever since double-entry bookkeeping was invented in the fifteenth century. Today their codifications are enforced by a vast institutional infrastructure made up of professional educators, public accounting firms, and regulatory bodies.

In contrast, efforts to measure market share, quality, innovation, human resources, and customer satisfaction have been much more modest. Data for tracking these measures are generated less often: quarterly, annual, or even biannual bases are common. Responsibility for them typically rests with a specific function. (Strategic planning measures market share, for example, while engineering measures innovation and so on.) They rarely become part of the periodic reports general managers receive.

Placing these new measures on an equal footing with financial data takes significant resources. One approach is to assign a senior executive to each of the measures and hold him or her responsible for developing its methodologies. Typically, these executives come from the function that is most experienced in dealing with the particular measure. But they work with a multifunctional task force to ensure that managers throughout the company will understand the resulting measures and find them useful. Another, less common, approach is to create a new function focused on one measure and then to expand its mandate over time. A unit responsible for customer satisfaction might subsequently take on market share, for example, or the company's performance in human resources.

Unlike a company's grammar, which should be fairly stable, methods for taking new performance measures should evolve as the company's expertise increases. Historical comparability may suffer in the process, but this is a minor loss. What matters is how a company is doing compared with its current competitors, not with its own past.

The last component of a corporate information architecture is the set of rules that governs the flow of information. Who is responsible for how measures are taken? Who actually generates the data? Who receives and analyzes them? Who is responsible for changing the rules? Because information is an important source of power, the way a company answers these questions matters deeply. How open or closed a company is affects how individuals and groups work together, as well as the relative influence people and parts of the company have on its strategic direction and management. Some companies make information available on a very limited basis. At others, any individual can request information from another unit as long as he or she can show why it is needed. Similarly, in some companies the CEO still determines who gets what information – not a very practical alternative in today's world. More often what happens is that those who possess information decide with whom they will share it.

Advances in information technology such as powerful workstations, open architectures, and relational databases vastly increase the options for how information can flow. It may be centralized at the top, so that senior executives can make even more decisions than they have in the past. Or it may be distributed to increase the decision-making responsibilities of people at every level. The advantages of making information widely available are obvious, though this also raises important questions that need to be addressed about the data's integrity and security. In principle, however, this portion of the information architecture ought to be the most flexible of the three, so that the company's information flows continue to change as the conditions it faces do.

Determining the hardware, software, and telecommunications technology a company needs to generate its new measurement information is the second activity in the performance revolution. This task is hard enough in its own right, given the many choices available. But too often managers make it even harder by going directly to a technology architecture without stopping first to think through their information needs. This was the case at a high-tech manufacturing company that was growing more and more frustrated with its information systems planning committee. Then the CEO realized that he and the other senior managers had not determined the measures they wanted before setting up the committee. Equipped with that information, the committee found it relatively easy to choose the right technology.

Once the information architecture and supporting technology are in place, the next step is to align the new system with the company's incentives – to reward people in proportion to their performance on the measures that management has said truly matter. This is easier said than done. In many companies, the compensation system limits the amount and range of the salary increases, bonuses, and stock options that management can award.

In companies that practice pay-for-performance, compensation and other rewards are often tied fairly mechanically to a few key financial measures such as profitability and return on investment. Convincing managers that a newly implemented system is really going to be followed can be a hard sell. The president of one service company let each of his division general managers design the performance measures that were most appropriate for his or her particular business. Even so, the managers still felt the bottom line was all that would matter when it came to promotions and pay.

The difficulty of aligning incentives to performance is heightened by the fact that formulas for

Formulas that tie incentives to performance look objective – and rarely work.

tying the two together are rarely effective. Formulas have the advantage of looking objective, and they spare managers the unpleasantness of having to conduct truly frank performance appraisals. But if the formula is simple and focuses on a few key variables, it inevitably leaves some important measures out. Conversely, if the formula is complex and factors in all the variables that require attention, people are likely to find it confusing and may start to play games with the numbers. Moreover, the relative importance of the variables is certain to change more often – and faster – than the whole incentive system can change.

For these reasons, I favor linking incentives strongly to performance but leaving managers free to determine their subordinates' rewards on the basis of all the relevant information, qualitative as well as quantitative. Then it is up to the manager to explain candidly to subordinates why they received what they did. For most managers, this will also entail learning to conduct effective performance appraisals, an indirect – and invaluable – benefit of overhauling the measurement system.

Outside parties such as industry and trade associations, third-party data vendors, information technology companies, consulting firms, and public accounting firms must also become part of the performance measurement revolution. Their incentive: important business opportunities.

Industry and trade associations can play a very helpful role in identifying key performance measures, researching methodologies for taking these measures, and supplying comparative statistics to their members – so can third-party data vendors. Competitors are more likely to supply information to a neutral party (which can disguise it and make it available to all its members or customers) than to

Public accounting firms have what may be the single most critical role in this revolution.

one another. And customers are more likely to provide information to a single data vendor than to each of their suppliers separately.

Consulting firms and information technology vendors also have important roles to play in forwarding the revolution. Firms that specialize in strategy formulation, for example, often have well-developed methods for assessing market share and other performance metrics that clients could be trained to use. Similarly, firms that focus on strategy implementation have a wealth of experience designing systems of various kinds for particular functions such as manufacturing and human resources. While many of these firms are likely to remain specialized, and thus require coordination by their clients, others will surely expand their capabilities to address all the pieces of the revolution within a client company.

Much the same thing is apt to happen among vendors of information technology. In addition to helping companies develop the technological architecture they need, some companies will see opportunities to move into a full range of services that use the hardware as a technology platform. IBM and DEC are already moving in this direction, impelled in part by the fact that dramatic gains in price-performance ratios make it harder and harder to make money selling "boxes."

Finally, public accounting firms have what may be the single most critical role in this revolution. On one hand, they could inhibit its progress in the belief that their vested interest in the existing system is too great to risk. On the other hand, all the large firms have substantial consulting practices, and the revolution represents a tremendous business opportunity for them. Companies will need a great deal of help developing new measures, validating them, and certifying them for external use.

Accounting firms also have an opportunity to develop measurement methods that will be common to an industry or across industries. While this should not be overdone, one reason financial measures carry such weight is that they are assumed to be a uniform metric, comparable across divisions and companies, and thus a valid basis for resource allocation decisions. In practice, of course, these measures are not comparable (despite the millions of hours invested in efforts to make them so) because companies use different accounting conventions. Given that fact, it is easy to see why developing additional measures that senior managers – and the investment community – can use will be a massive undertaking.

Indeed, the power of research analysts and investors generally is one of the reasons accounting firms have such a crucial role to play. Although evidence exists that investors are showing more interest in metrics such as market share and cash flow, many managers and analysts identify the investment community as the chief impediment to revolution.[5] Until investors treat other measures as seriously as financial data, they argue, limits will always exist on how seriously those measures are taken inside companies.

GE's experience with its measurement task force supports their argument. According to a knowledgeable senior executive, the 1951 effort had only a modest effect because the measures believed to determine the company's stock price, to which incen-

Would managers be willing to publish anything more than the financial information the SEC requires?

tives were tied, were all financial: earnings per share, return on equity, return on investment, return on sales, and earnings growth rate. He believed that once the financial markets valued other measures, progress within companies would accelerate.

Investors, of course, see the problem from a different perspective. They question whether managers would be willing to publish anything more than the financial information required by the SEC lest they reveal too much to their competitors. Ultimately, a regulatory body like the SEC could untie this Gordian knot by recommending (and eventually requiring) public companies to provide nonfinancial measures in their reports. (This is, after all, how financial

5. "Investors: Look at Firms' Market Share," *Wall Street Journal*, February 26, 1990, pp. C1-2.

standards became so omnipotent and why so many millions of hours have been invested in their development.) But I suspect competitive pressure will prove a more immediate force for change. As soon as one leading company can demonstrate the long-term advantage of its superior performance on quality or innovation or any other nonfinancial measure, it will change the rules for all its rivals forever. And with so many serious competitors tracking – and enhancing – these measures, that is only a matter of time.

Designing a process to ensure that all these things happen is the last aspect of the revolution. To overcome conservative forces outside the company and from within (including line and staff managers at every level, in every function), someone has to take the lead. Ultimately, this means the CEO. If the CEO is not committed, the revolution will flounder, no matter how much enthusiasm exists throughout the organization.

But the CEO cannot make it happen. Developing an information architecture and its accompanying technology, aligning incentives, working with outside parties – all this requires many people and a lot of work, much of it far less interesting than plotting strategy. Moreover, the design of the process must take account of the integrative nature of the task: people in different businesses and functions including strategic planning, engineering, manufacturing, marketing and sales, human resources, and finance will all have something to contribute. The work of external players will have to be integrated with the company's own efforts.

Organizationally, two critical choices exist. One is who the point person will be. Assigning this role to the CEO or president ensures its proper symbolic visibility. Delegating it to a high-level line or staff executive and making it a big piece of his or her assignment may be a more effective way to guarantee that enough senior management time will be devoted to the project.

The other choice is which function or group will do most of the work and coordinate the company's efforts. The CEO of one high-tech company gave this responsibility to the finance function because he felt they should have the opportunity to broaden their perspective and measurement skills. He also thought it would be easier to use an existing group experienced in performance measurement. The president of an apparel company made a different choice. To avoid the financial bias embedded in the company's existing management information systems, he wanted someone to start from scratch and design a system with customer service at its core. As a result, he is planning to combine the information systems department with customer service to create a new function to be headed by a new person, recruited from the outside.

What is most effective for a given company will depend on its history, culture, and management style. But every company should make the effort to attack the problem with new principles. Some past practices may still be useful, but everything should be strenuously challenged. Otherwise, the effort will yield incremental changes at best.

Open-mindedness about the structures and processes that will be most effective, now and in the future, is equally important. I know of a few companies that are experimenting with combining the information systems and human resource depart-

> Combining information systems and human resources is a culture shock for both departments. But that's what revolution is all about.

ments. These experiments have entailed a certain amount of culture shock for professionals from both functions, but such radical rethinking is what revolution is all about.

Finally, recognize that once begun, this is a revolution that never ends. We are not simply talking about changing the basis of performance measurement from financial statistics to something else. We are talking about a new philosophy of performance measurement that regards it as an ongoing, evolving process. And just as igniting the revolution will take special effort, so will maintaining its momentum – and reaping the rewards in the years ahead. ▽

Reprint 91103

Measuring profit center managers

John Dearden

Many large companies still measure the financial performance of their profit center managers with techniques developed in the 1920s. They are based on return on investment. In this age of fast-paced change in both technology and management information systems, the attachment to these systems is not only strange but debilitating. Over the past 20 years, I've discussed the problem with senior and division managers both here and abroad and found that, while they recognize the difficulties such systemic rigidities impose, they do not know how to change their systems.

How you measure the performance of your managers directly affects the way they act.

Before management can build a new system, it must understand what is wrong with the old one. I have discovered that the use of return on investment is symptomatic of other, basic conceptual errors in profit center measurement systems. These errors are:

1   The failure to distinguish between techniques used to measure past financial performance and those required to establish future performance objectives.

2   The failure to differentiate between systems that measure the performance of the profit center and those that measure the performance of its managers.

3   The failure to segment variances from the budget by differences in the way that managers can influence them.

In this article I will describe the basis for these conceptual errors, explain how they result in suboptimal measurement systems, and suggest action management can take to correct the problems the systems create.

Conceptual flaws

In using traditional accounting systems to measure organizational units' performance, companies judge the adequacy of profits by comparing the amounts earned during a series of time periods and calculating the rates of return on the investments made.

Most companies emulate the systems that Du Pont and General Motors developed in the 1920s. Both businesses decentralized profit responsibility to operating units and at the same time began to use ROI to measure their units' financial performance. They expressed future profit objectives in terms of return on divisional assets and began to base projected performance on past results. Later they formalized these ROI objectives into profit budgets.

Measuring vs. projecting

Return on investment is a valid technique for measuring past profitability. In fact, it is the

John Dearden is the Herman C. Krannert Professor of Business Administration at the Harvard Business School. A recognized authority on both control and management information systems, he has written many books and articles on these subjects. This is his twenty-second contribution to HBR.

only technique that allows a company to compare profitability among organizations or investments. But it is not a valid way to set future objectives, because the historical costs of assets—on which it is based—are meaningless in planning future action. Regardless of how much a company pays for a group of assets or what amount of differential cash flow it projects in investment proposals, the only logical thing its managers can do—once the assets are in place—is to use the assets to maximize future cash flow and to invest in new assets when the return from these assets is expected to equal or exceed the company's cost of capital. The failure to make this distinction—between measuring the past and projecting the future—is the principal reason that companies continue to use ROI to measure the financial performance of their managers.

Not making this distinction adds to the undesirable side effects already inherent in ROI as managers try to maximize their return on investment. (For a summary of these side effects, please see the insert "How ROI Can Hurt.")

Not only are historical accounting values of existing fixed assets not relevant, but as soon as a new asset is added, neither the cost nor the projected savings are relevant to future planning except to ascertain how well estimates have been made.

Companies should express profit objectives for both the profit center and its manager in terms of absolute dollars of profit, which are based on the projected potential of existing resources to generate cash flow.

The manager vs. the profit center

Current systems also fail to distinguish explicitly between the measurement of the financial performance of a manager and that of the organizational unit being managed. It is important to make this distinction because:

☐   A company can measure a profit center's financial performance only in absolute terms, while it can measure the unit's head only in relative terms. Managers' performance is limited by their own units' profit potential. Otherwise, managers of high-profit divisions would always be considered successful and managers of low-profit divisions, marginal or unsuccessful.

☐   The extent to which a manager can control an item of revenue or expense is irrelevant to measuring a profit center's performance. For example, the impact of foreign exchange translation gains or losses is important to evaluating a subsidiary's profitability. This impact is entirely irrelevant, however, to judging the performance of that subsidiary's manager.

Many multinationals measure foreign subsidiary managers on the basis of the American dollar, so when the dollar goes up, the performance of the subsidiary goes down. Senior managers believe that tying the foreign subsidiary managers to the dollar forces them to make up for shortfalls in other areas, so that the impact on the corporation as a whole is neutral. But the impact on the manager is very real and demotivating. Managers abroad rightly complain to headquarters that they have no influence on the very factors with which they are being judged.

From the company's point of view, this tie to the dollar may force managers to make up for the problems themselves, but it also gives managers a screen behind which to hide mistakes. When the dollar goes down, the subsidiary's performance goes up, no matter what. Poorly run divisions have been able to hide their failures for years when the dollar has been weak.

☐   The methods used to measure managers affect the way they act. If companies measure ROI, their managers will do all they can to optimize the ratio, and that may result in suboptimal decisions.

Of course few, if any, companies do measure managers in absolute terms. Almost all companies measure managers against profit budgets, which should take into account the potential profitability of the resources being managed. But by using a single system to measure both the organizational unit and its manager, the company includes items that are irrelevant to management performance and may also exclude items that *are* relevant. The performance criteria for the profit center (return on investment, for example) differ from those for the manager (actual profit compared with budgeted profit, for instance).

I believe that companies should separate their measurement systems and use the traditional accounting system for profit center financial statements and separate profit budget reports to measure managers.

Segmenting variances from the budget

Most companies begin the budgeting process by reviewing a strategic plan. The strategic planning process, of course, affects the profit budget. The financial aspects of the strategic plan must be in terms of future cash flow; historical costs are not important to the plan. And the plan is for the profit center, not its manager. Only when the company converts

"I suppose the rest of us are to consider ourselves redundant!"

the plan's first year into a detailed profit budget does the manager's responsibility become clear.

In formulating a better profit budget, top management must decide for which items profit center managers are to be held responsible and the degree to which they must meet specific goals. Very few items are entirely controllable by managers, but very few items cannot be influenced by managers. It is important to remember that the distinction is *not* controllability but the ability to influence.

The company should not automatically consider favorable variances good and unfavorable ones bad. It can judge good or poor performance only after it analyzes variances against management explanation.

I propose as a guideline for drawing up the profit budget that the company include only items that managers can influence. Profit center managers are, then, responsible for doing their best to meet or exceed this goal and for explaining the reasons for any variances and what they are doing to correct unfavorable variances.

In general, I believe a profit center manager can influence and thus be held responsible for:

1   All profit and loss items generated directly by the profit center.
2   Any expense incurred outside the center at headquarters or other units for which the center can be billed directly.
3   An expense equal to the controllable working capital (usually receivables and inventories less payables) multiplied by an interest rate (the company's marginal borrowing rate, for instance). I believe

such a charge is necessary to take into account trade-offs between the levels of working capital and profits. For example, higher inventories can reduce losses from stock-outs, and liberalized credit terms can result in higher sales. Only the profit center manager knows and understands these trade-offs. Because conditions are constantly changing, it is usually not effective to budget working capital levels. The charge will motivate managers to make these trade-offs in the company's best interests. If managers can increase profits above the costs of carrying receivables and inventories, the company will benefit.

In the same spirit, the company would replace depreciation based on historical cost with an amount equal to depreciation based on replacement cost. Depreciation, like the book value of fixed assets, is generally irrelevant to budgeting because a company is primarily concerned with maximizing cash flow. Being a sunk cost, depreciation does not affect the measurement of a profit center's performance.

Depreciation is important in product profitability analysis, however, where management diagnoses areas that are doing well versus those that are doing poorly. Each product varies widely in its use of capital; to gauge profitability, it is necessary to include the replacement costs of the assets used in calculating depreciation.

ROI is the wrong way to measure how well profit center managers perform.

Under my proposal, the budgeted amount and the actual amount in the budget report would be the same, so depreciation would not affect performance. In fact, managers could omit depreciation from their reports and still calculate their products' profitability. If included, this figure will get greater visibility and consequently will more likely be used.

I advocate a profit budget expressed in terms of dollars to be earned in the budget year. The amount should represent the best estimate of the profit center's potential cash flow as developed through the strategic planning process. The profit budget will include only the parts of the plan a manager can influence. It is the manager's personal financial goal. The manager must explain any deviations from it.

Reporting against budget

I would divide the reporting system that accompanies the budgeting system into three parts: (1) an analysis of variances from budget, (2) an explanation of the causes of those variances and any corrective action being taken, and (3) a forecast for the year. Many senior executives have trouble getting realistic (or even honest) explanations and forecasts from profit center managers, especially when the variances are unfavorable. The worse the variance, the greater the danger of cover-up.

This serious problem can be solved if profit center managers know precisely what their financial objectives are and are tested against only the income and expense they can influence. By organizing the analysis to separate variances by the degree of management responsibility, the company will increase the reliability and accuracy of the budget reports.

In most profit budget reporting systems, companies do not classify variances explicitly by the degree of influence management has on them. The practice leads to considerable ambiguity in the explanation of variances and the evaluation of performance. The report should indicate the difference in the degree of influence that a profit center manager can exert on each variance. If a company treats all variances as if they were homogeneous, it may perceive a favorable variance on which the manager has little influence as an offset to an unfavorable variance on which the manager has considerable influence.

Instead, companies should classify variances according to whether they are forecast, performance, or discretionary cost variances.

Forecast variances

I have found some confusion over the difference between a budget and a forecast, which some managers tend to treat as the same thing. A budget is not a forecast. A budget is a management plan and is based on the assumption that steps will be taken to make events correspond to the plan. A forecast is a prediction of what will most likely happen and carries no implication that the forecaster will attempt to shape events to realize the forecast. A projection is not a prediction but an estimate of what will happen if various conditions and situations exist.

The typical profit budget includes many forecasts. A company should treat them separately because it should judge managers solely on their ability to manage—not on their ability to forecast.

Perhaps the most important forecast in a typical profit budget is that of the total level of sales activity expected in the industry during the budget period. Everybody knows that swings in industry volume can sometimes affect profits to such a degree that all other variances appear minor in comparison.

By isolating the industry volume variance, you can more easily evaluate its impact—see that the volume is going down, for example, but that the manager is increasing market penetration. The industry volume variance allows you to see that the manager is doing well despite adverse conditions.

Managers have no control over swings in industry volume— and should not have to answer for them.

Each budget also forecasts the level of purchase prices on such costs as raw materials, utilities, supplies, and wages and salaries. The profit center manager normally has little, if any, influence over them. It is also necessary to forecast the level of selling prices, another item over which the manager has limited control. If, however, the budget were to combine purchase and sales price variances, they should offset each other because changes in the purchase prices should affect selling prices. Profit center managers *can* influence the effect of price level cost changes on profitability.

Performance variances

These variances include market share and operating costs. Because the manager can affect his or her unit's market share and its efficiency, they are the two most important variances a company can use to evaluate the profit center manager. Moreover, they are the most concrete, for they leave the manager little room for ambiguity in explaining them.

In manufacturing profit centers, the most important performance variables are materials usage, direct labor, and overhead. In a service industry like a clothing chain, the actual costs of operating the stores,

How ROI can hurt

I have found that using return on investment to measure profit center managers causes corporate problems because:

☐
The emphasis is on optimizing a ratio, which could discourage growth in the most profitable divisions. Investments in high profit divisions may lower their return, while the same investment in low profit divisions could improve it.

☐
Investments that might earn satisfactory returns will not do so at first because ROI requires that the investments be increased by the total gross book value of the new assets. Managers may not invest if they expect their tenure to be short. Also, their returns will increase over time if they don't make new investments.

☐
All assets in the same division, whether special-purpose assets, general-purpose assets, or working capital, must earn the same rate of return. Moreover, this rate of return is often inconsistent with the company's cost of capital.

☐
The same assets in different divisions may have different implicit interest rates, which may lead to different inventory decision rules in different divisions for identical items of inventory.

☐
Under certain conditions, division managers can increase their rate of return by scrapping perfectly good assets.

less the budgeted costs, are important performance variables.

Performance variables measure the profit center's level of efficiency and effectiveness. The profit center manager agrees to go after a given market share and to operate at a certain level of efficiency.

Discretionary expense variances

These expenses include administration, marketing, and research and development. Variances in these expenses indicate only whether more or less money has been spent than originally budgeted. They do not indicate efficiency or inefficiency, as other variances do. A company must segregate discretionary expense variances from the others because managers should not offset unfavorable performance with favorable discretionary expense variances. A company wants to avoid a situation in which a profit center manager takes bud-

geted objectives so seriously that he or she cuts back on marketing or product development costs to compensate for unfavorable manufacturing cost variances.

The bottom line

In most decentralized companies, managers are under pressure to meet current goals. This pressure influences them to cover up bad news and to take short-term action that is not in the long-run interests of their companies. A system that holds managers responsible for what they really can influence and allows them to explain the reasons they cannot achieve certain goals will relieve some of this pressure. Managers feel freer to communicate bad news if their goals are clear and unambiguous and they know they will be measured on the variances from items for which they are clearly responsible.

The evaluation of subordinates is one of the most important responsibilities of senior management, if not *the* most important one. Evaluation usually involves the observation of a manager's performance over a period normally exceeding the year covered by the typical profit budget. The evaluation also involves measuring managers on several dimensions in addition to their financial performance. Even the best short-term financial measurement systems do not ensure fair evaluation. Without such systems, however, evaluations are much more likely to be unsatisfactory and profit center managers much more likely to take action contrary to the best interests of their companies.

It is difficult to change a financial measurement system that has been in place for a number of years. Generally, almost everyone involved—from the controller to the profit center manager—will resist change. The managers responsible are often reluctant to change because change implies that the current systems are defective. Profit center managers usually believe they can work within the present systems and are unsure of the new. But change is worth the effort necessary to achieve it.

It is quite easy to diagnose the potential problems many current measurement systems create and even easier to decide what corrective actions to take. The problem is not what to do but how to do it.

Companies cannot afford to continue to use the techniques developed in the 1920s to measure the performance of profit center managers in the 1980s. A system of evaluation that is less ambiguous will be more fair to everyone, but it is hard to start the process of change. Unless innovative senior managers begin, however, they will continue to demotivate performance instead of measure it. ▽

Reprint 87503

READ THE FINE PRINT

REPRINTS
Telephone: 617-495-6192
Fax: 617-495-6985

Current and past articles are available, as is an annually updated index. Discounts apply to large-quantity purchases.

Please send orders to
HBR Reprints
Harvard Business School
Publishing Division
Boston, MA 02163.

HOW CAN *HARVARD BUSINESS REVIEW* ARTICLES WORK FOR YOU?

For years, we've printed a microscopically small notice on the editorial credits page of the *Harvard Business Review* alerting our readers to the availability of *HBR* articles.

Now we invite you to take a closer look at some of the many ways you can put this hard-working business tool to work for you.

IN THE CORPORATE CLASSROOM.

There's no more effective, or cost-effective, way to supplement your corporate training programs than in-depth, incisive *HBR* articles.

Affordable and accessible, it's no wonder hundreds of companies and consulting organizations use *HBR* articles as a centerpiece for management training.

IN-BOX INNOVATION.

Where do your company's movers and shakers get their big ideas? Many find the inspiration for innovation in the pages of *HBR*. They then share the wealth and spread the word by distributing *HBR* articles to company colleagues.

IN MARKETING AND SALES SUPPORT.

HBR articles are a substantive leave-behind to your sales calls. And they can add credibility to your direct mail campaigns. They demonstrate that your company is on the leading edge of business thinking.

CREATE CUSTOM ARTICLES.

If you want to pack even greater power in your punch, personalize *HBR* articles with your company's name or logo. And get the added benefit of putting your organization's name before your customers.

AND THERE ARE 500 MORE REASONS IN THE *HBR CATALOG.*

In all, the *Harvard Business Review Catalog* lists articles on over 500 different subjects. Plus, you'll find books and videos on subjects you need to know.

The catalog is yours for just $8.00. To order *HBR* articles or the *HBR Catalog* (No. 21019), call 617-495-6192. Please mention telephone order code 025A when placing your order. Or FAX us at 617-495-6985.

And start putting *HBR* articles to work for you.

**Harvard Business School
Publications**

Call 617-495-6192 to order the *HBR Catalog.*

(Prices and terms subject to change.)